## INTRODUCTION

Welcome to the world of digital publishing ~ the book you now hold in your hand, while unchanged from the original **1970** edition, was printed using the latest state of the art digital technology. The advent of print-on-demand has forever changed the publishing process, never has information been so accessible and it is our hope that this book serves your informational needs for years to come. If this is your first exposure to digital publishing, we hope that you are pleased with the results. Many more titles of interest to the classic automobile and motorcycle enthusiast, collector and restorer are available via our website at **www.VelocePress.com.** We hope that you find this title as interesting as we do.

## NOTE FROM THE PUBLISHER

The information presented is true and complete to the best of our knowledge. All recommendations are made without any guarantees on the part of the author or the publisher, who also disclaim all liability incurred with the use of this information.

## TRADEMARKS

We recognize that some words, model names and designations, for example, mentioned herein are the property of the trademark holder. We use them for identification purposes only. This is not an official publication.

## INFORMATION ON THE USE OF THIS PUBLICATION

This manual is an invaluable resource for the classic **SUZUKI** enthusiast and a "must have" for owners interested in performing their own maintenance. However, in today's information age we are constantly subject to changes in common practice, new technology, availability of improved materials and increased awareness of chemical toxicity. As such, it is advised that the user consult with an experienced professional prior to undertaking any procedure described herein. While every care has been taken to ensure correctness of information, it is obviously not possible to guarantee complete freedom from errors or omissions or to accept liability arising from such errors or omissions. Therefore, any individual that uses the information contained within, or elects to perform or participate in do-it-yourself repairs or modifications acknowledges that there is a risk factor involved and that the publisher or its associates cannot be held responsible for personal injury or property damage resulting from the use of the information or the outcome of such procedures.

It is important that the reader recognizes that any instructions may refer to either the right-hand or left-hand sides of the vehicle or the components and that the directions are followed carefully. One final word of advice, this publication is intended to be used as a reference guide, and when in doubt the reader should consult with a qualified technician.

**www.VelocePress.com**

# SUZUKI
# T10 - 250cc
# OWNERS HANDBOOK
# and SERVICE MANUAL

1964 MODEL T10

originally
published by

**FLOYD CLYMER PUBLICATIONS**
World's Largest Publisher of Books Relating to Automobiles, Motorcycles, Motor Racing, and Americana
222 NO. VIRGIL AVE., LOS ANGELES, CALIFORNIA 90004

# Message from the Publisher

There are actually two books in one in this Suzuki Shop Manual and Handbook. Owners, dealers, mechanics, enthusiasts and collectors will find it most useful.

With the cooperation of U. S. Suzuki Motor Corporation, we arranged to reprint for the U. S. market their shop manual - exactly as originally printed in Japan. There are, as in manuals compiled and printed in foreign countries, some expressions quite different than we would use, which is intriguing and interesting.

Suzuki has made a great name for itself in the few short years that this popular Japanese make has been imported and sold in the United States. They have thousands of loyal and satisfied owners in the U. S. as well as in other countries throughout the world. They have a substantial group of Suzuki dealers and, while this book is extremely informative, we suggest that the Suzuki owner patronize his authorized Suzuki dealer when in need of service. The dealer has not only the proper and necessary tools, but geniune parts and mechanics trained in the proper servicing of Suzuki machines.

For the name of your nearest Suzuki dealer and other information, we suggest that you write to U. S. Suzuki Motor Corporation, 13767 Freeway Drive, Santa Fe Springs, Calif. 90670, as they are factory-owned and controlled.

If this book does not cover your model, please write us as additional Suzuki books will be available soon. We are happy to add this interesting book to our large list of over 400 titles on cars and motorcycles - and more are coming every month. Send for free catalog of our entire list.

We hope you like the book.

*Floyd Clymer*

**FLOYD CLYMER PUBLICATIONS**
*World's Largest Publisher of Books Relating to Automobiles, Motorcycles, Motor Racing, and Americana*
222 NO. VIRGIL AVE., LOS ANGELES, CALIFORNIA 90004

# SUZUKI MANUAL

## Book 1

Owners Handbook
and Service Manual
for Model T10

# CONTENTS

| | |
|---|---|
| SPECIFICATIONS | 8 |
| PERFORMANCE CURVES | 10 |
| SPECIAL TOOLS | 11 |
| FUEL MIXTURE | 12 |
| TROUBLE SHOOTING | 12 |
| ENGINE | |
|   1. Removing Engine from Frame | 22 |
|   2. Disassembly | 23 |
|     A. Work which Can Be Done with Engine in Frame | 23 |
|     B. Work for which Engine Must Be Removed from Frame | 23 |
|     C. Disassembling | 23 |
|   3. Assembling | 31 |
|     A. Engine Assembling Tips | 31 |
|     B. Tools, Etc. | 31 |
|     C. Tips on Tightening Nuts and Bolts | 31 |
|     D. Assembling Procedure | 31 |
|     E. Applying Liquid Gasket | 32 |
|     F. Installing Transmission Gears | 32 |
|     G. Speedometer Drive Gear | 32 |
|     H. Dowel Pins, Slotted Bearing Positioning Pieces | 33 |
|     I. Installing Crankshaft Assembly | 33 |
|     J. Tips on Installing Countershaft and Drive Shaft | 33 |
|     K. Testing Transmission Gears | 34 |
|     L. Tips on Fitting Lower Crankcase | 34 |
|     M. Tightening Crankcase Bolts | 34 |
|     N. Installing Oil Reservoir Caps, Change Lever, Kick Starter Parts | 34 |
|     O. Installing Clutch Push Rods | 35 |
|     P. Installing Electrical Equipment | 36 |
|     Q. Installing Cylinders | 36 |
|   4. Engine Construction and Inspections | 36 |
|     A. Combustion System | 36 |
|       (1) Cylinder Heads | 36 |
|       (2) Head Gaskets | 36 |
|       (3) Cylinders | 37 |
|       (4) Pistons | 38 |
|       (5) Piston Rings | 39 |
|       (6) Inspecting Piston Ring Wear and Tension | 39 |
|       (7) Piston Pins | 41 |
|       (8) Crankcase | 41 |
|     B. Power Transmission System | 41 |
|       (1) Clutch | 41 |
|       (2) Inspecting Clutch Springs | 42 |
|       (3) Inspecting Clutch Plates | 42 |
|       (4) Inspecting Clutch Sleeve Hub | 43 |
|       (5) Inspecting Clutch Housing | 44 |
|       (6) Transmission | 44 |
|       (7) Kick Starter | 45 |
|     C. Fuel System | 45 |
|       (1) Carburetors | 45 |
|         (A) Operation | 46 |

|     |       | (B) | Specifications | 46 |
|---|---|---|---|---|
|     |       | (C) | Construction | 46 |
|     |       |     | a. Main Channel | 46 |
|     |       |     | b. Slow Channel | 46 |
|     |       | (D) | Cleaning Carburetors | 46 |
|     |       |     | a. Removing | 46 |
|     |       |     | b. Disassembling | 46 |
|     |       |     | c. Inspecting and Servicing | 47 |
|     |       |     | d. Assembling | 47 |
|     |       |     | e. Installing | 47 |
|     |       | (E) | Tips on Mounting Carburetors | 47 |
|     |       | (F) | Adjusting Idling | 48 |
|     |       |     | a. Preparations | 48 |
|     |       |     | b. Adjusting | 48 |
|     |       |     | c. Balancing Right and Left Cylinders | 48 |
|     |       | (G) | Adjusting Fuel/Air Mixture | 48 |
|     |       |     | a. Too Rich Fuel | 48 |
|     |       |     | b. Too Lean Fuel | 48 |
|     |       | (H) | Adjusting Carburetor for All Speeds | 49 |
|     |       |     | a. Adjusting for High Speeds | 49 |
|     |       |     | b. Adjusting for Medium Speeds | 49 |
|     |       |     | • Adjusting with Jet Needle | 49 |
|     |       |     | • Adjusting with Throttle Valve Cutaway | 49 |
|     |       |     | c. Adjusting for Low Speeds | 49 |
|     |       | (I) | Carburetor Adjusting Chart | 49 |
|     |   (2) | Throttle Cable Connector | | 49 |
|     |       | (A) | Construction | 49 |
|     |   (3) | Adjusting Throttle Cables | | 49 |

FRAME

1. Inspecting and Servicing Frame . . . . . . . . . . . . . . . . . . . . 50
    A. Twist and Alignment Inspection . . . . . . . . . . . . . . . . . 50
    B. Ball Races and Steel Balls . . . . . . . . . . . . . . . . . . . 50
        (1) Installing Ball Races . . . . . . . . . . . . . . . . . . . 50
2. Tires . . . . . . . . . . . . . . . . . . . . . . . . . . . . . . . . 51
    A. Removing and Fitting Tires and Inner Tubes . . . . . . . . . . . 52
3. Air Cleaners . . . . . . . . . . . . . . . . . . . . . . . . . . . . 52
4. Exhaust System . . . . . . . . . . . . . . . . . . . . . . . . . . . 53
5. Dual Seat . . . . . . . . . . . . . . . . . . . . . . . . . . . . . . 53
6. Fuel Tank and Fuel Cock . . . . . . . . . . . . . . . . . . . . . . . 53
    A. Removing . . . . . . . . . . . . . . . . . . . . . . . . . . . . 54
    B. Inspecting and Servicing . . . . . . . . . . . . . . . . . . . . 54
7. Speedometer . . . . . . . . . . . . . . . . . . . . . . . . . . . . . 55
    A. Speed Indicator . . . . . . . . . . . . . . . . . . . . . . . . 55
    B. Distance Meter . . . . . . . . . . . . . . . . . . . . . . . . . 55
8. Hydraulic Brake . . . . . . . . . . . . . . . . . . . . . . . . . . . 55
    A. Comparison of Mechanical and Hydraulic Brakes . . . . . . . . . 55
        (1) Mechanical Brake . . . . . . . . . . . . . . . . . . . . . 55
        (2) Hydraulic Brake . . . . . . . . . . . . . . . . . . . . . . 55
    B. Master Cylinder . . . . . . . . . . . . . . . . . . . . . . . . 56
        (1) Construction . . . . . . . . . . . . . . . . . . . . . . . 56

|  |  |  |  |
|---|---|---|---|
| | (2) | Operation | 57 |
| | (3) | Removing | 58 |
| | (4) | Disassembling | 58 |
| | (5) | Tips on Handling | 58 |
| | (6) | Tips on Assembling | 59 |
| | (7) | Assembling | 59 |
| | (8) | Installing | 59 |
| | (9) | Inspection after Installation | 60 |
| | (10) | Adjustment and Maintenance Standards | 60 |
| | | (A) Master Cylinder | 60 |
| | | (B) Master Cylinder Cap | 60 |
| | | (C) Master Piston | 60 |
| | | (D) Master Piston Valve and Oil Seal | 60 |
| | | (E) Master Piston Valve Spacer | 60 |
| | | (F) Master Piston Outlet Valve and Outlet Valve Seat Gasket | 60 |
| | | (G) Master Piston Return Spring | 60 |
| | | (H) Master Cylinder Union Bolt | 60 |
| | | (I) Master Piston Stopper | 60 |
| | | (J) Master Cylinder Cap Gasket and Union Gaskets | 61 |
| | | (K) Master Cylinder Boot | 61 |
| | | (L) Master Piston Push Rod | 61 |
| C. | Rear Brake Cylinder | | 61 |
| | (1) | Construction | 61 |
| | (2) | Operation | 61 |
| | (3) | Tips on Handling | 61 |
| | (4) | Adjustment and Maintenance Standards | 62 |
| | | (A) Rear Brake Cylinder | 62 |
| | | (B) Rear Brake Cylinder Piston | 62 |
| | | (C) Rear Brake Cylinder Oil Seals | 62 |
| | | (D) Rear Brake Cylinder Oil Seal Spring | 62 |
| | | (E) Rear Brake Cylinder Dust Seal | 63 |
| | | (F) Rear Brake Cylinder Union Bolt | 63 |
| | | (G) Rear Brake Cylinder Bleeder Valve | 63 |
| | | (H) Rear Brake Cylinder Bleeder Pipe | 63 |
| | | (I) Rear Brake Cylinder Union Gaskets | 63 |
| | | (J) Bleeder Valve Cap | 63 |
| | (5) | Rear Brake Adjustments and Maintenance Standards | 63 |
| | | (A) Rear Hub Panel | 63 |
| | | (B) Brake Shoes | 63 |
| | | (C) Rear Hub | 63 |
| | | (D) Brake Shoe Return Springs | 63 |
| | | (E) Rear Brake Shoe Adjuster Cam Shaft | 63 |
| | (6) | Tips on Installing Brake Hose | 63 |
| D. | Hydraulic Brake Oil | | 63 |
| | (1) | Tips on Handling | 64 |
| | (2) | New Motorcycle Service | 64 |
| E. | Adjusting Hydraulic Brake | | 64 |
| | (1) | Adjusting Rear Brake Shoe Clearance | 64 |
| | (2) | Adjusting Brake Pedal Play | 65 |
| | (3) | Clearance between Push Rod and Master Piston | 65 |

(4) Removing Air from Hydraulic Brake System . . . . . . . . . . 65
(5) Changing Brake Oil . . . . . . . . . . . . . . . . . . . . 66
F. Daily Inspection . . . . . . . . . . . . . . . . . . . . . . . 66
G. Periodic Inspection . . . . . . . . . . . . . . . . . . . . . 66
(1) Tips on Periodic Inspection . . . . . . . . . . . . . . . . 66
H. Hydraulic Brake Trouble Causes and Repairs . . . . . . . . . . 66
(1) If Rear Brake Drags . . . . . . . . . . . . . . . . . . . 66
(2) Insufficient Braking and Large Brake Pedal Travel . . . . . . . 67
(3) Abnormal Noise in Brake . . . . . . . . . . . . . . . . . . 67
I. Tips on Handling Hydraulic Brake . . . . . . . . . . . . . . . 67
J. Removing Rear Wheel . . . . . . . . . . . . . . . . . . . . . 68
K. Inspection and Service . . . . . . . . . . . . . . . . . . . . 68
9. Front Brake . . . . . . . . . . . . . . . . . . . . . . . . . . 69
A. Disassembling . . . . . . . . . . . . . . . . . . . . . . . . 69
B. Assembling . . . . . . . . . . . . . . . . . . . . . . . . . . 70
C. Brake Drum and Brake Lining . . . . . . . . . . . . . . . . . . 70
D. Inspecting and Replacing Wheel Bearings and Hub Drum Oil Seals . . 70
(1) Tips on Installing Bearings . . . . . . . . . . . . . . . . . 71
(2) Inspecting Bearings . . . . . . . . . . . . . . . . . . . . 71
10. Inspecting Rim Shake . . . . . . . . . . . . . . . . . . . . . 71
11. Wheel Alignment . . . . . . . . . . . . . . . . . . . . . . . 71
12. Front Fork . . . . . . . . . . . . . . . . . . . . . . . . . . 72
A. Disassembling . . . . . . . . . . . . . . . . . . . . . . . . 72
B. Inspection and Servicing . . . . . . . . . . . . . . . . . . . 72
C. Assembling . . . . . . . . . . . . . . . . . . . . . . . . . . 72
13. Steering Stem . . . . . . . . . . . . . . . . . . . . . . . . . 74
A. Disassembling . . . . . . . . . . . . . . . . . . . . . . . . 74
B. Inspection and Servicing . . . . . . . . . . . . . . . . . . . 75
C. Assembling . . . . . . . . . . . . . . . . . . . . . . . . . . 75
ELECTRICAL EQUIPMENT
1. Charging System . . . . . . . . . . . . . . . . . . . . . . . . 76
A. Starter Dynamo . . . . . . . . . . . . . . . . . . . . . . . . 76
(1) Specifications . . . . . . . . . . . . . . . . . . . . . . 76
(2) Construction . . . . . . . . . . . . . . . . . . . . . . . 76
(3) Operation . . . . . . . . . . . . . . . . . . . . . . . . . 77
(4) Inspection and Adjustments . . . . . . . . . . . . . . . . . 77
(A) Inspection every 500 km (300 miles) . . . . . . . . . . 77
(B) Inspection every 3,000 km (1,900 miles) . . . . . . . . 77
(C) Inspection every 5,000, 7,000 and 10,000 km (3,000, 4,500 and 6,000 miles) . . . . . . . . . . . . . . . . 78
(5) Dynamo Trouble Shooting . . . . . . . . . . . . . . . . . . 78
(A) If Starter Does Not Turn or Battery Is Not Charged Properly . . . . . . . . . . . . . . . . . . . . . . 78
(B) If Battery Is Not Charged . . . . . . . . . . . . . . 78
2. Ignition System . . . . . . . . . . . . . . . . . . . . . . . . 79
A. Operation . . . . . . . . . . . . . . . . . . . . . . . . . . . 79
B. Construction of Ignition Coil . . . . . . . . . . . . . . . . . 79
(1) Inspection . . . . . . . . . . . . . . . . . . . . . . . . 80
C. Contact Breaker . . . . . . . . . . . . . . . . . . . . . . . . 80
D. Condenser . . . . . . . . . . . . . . . . . . . . . . . . . . . 80

|  |  |  |  |
|---|---|---|---|
| | E. Timing Advancer | | 80 |
| | F. Spark Plugs | | 81 |
| | (1) Construction | | 81 |
| | (2) Heat Range | | 81 |
| | (3) Conversion Chart | | 82 |
| 3. | Safety Devices | | 82 |
| | A. Turn Signal Relay | | 82 |
| | B. Horn | | 82 |
| | (1) Construction | | 82 |
| | (2) Operation | | 83 |
| | C. Battery | | 83 |
| | (1) Specifications | | 83 |
| | (2) Construction | | 84 |
| | (A) Positive Plates | | 84 |
| | (B) Negative Plates | | 84 |
| | (C) Insulators | | 84 |
| | (D) Fiberglass Mats | | 84 |
| | (E) Cells | | 84 |
| | (F) Electrolyte | | 84 |
| | (3) Operation | | 84 |
| | (4) Capacity | | 85 |
| | (5) Capacity and Solution Temperature | | 86 |
| | (6) Adding to Solution | | 86 |
| | (7) Auto-Discharge | | 86 |
| | (8) Initial Charging | | 86 |
| | (A) How to Charge | | 86 |

PERIODICAL SERVICING
1. Adjusting Ignition Timing . . . 88
   A. Left Cylinder . . . 88
   B. Right Cylinder . . . 88
   C. Adjusting Timing with Gauge . . . 88
      (1) Timing Gauge . . . 89
2. Cleaning Spark Plugs and Adjusting Gap . . . 89
3. Adjusting Clutch . . . 90
4. Servicing Brakes . . . 90
   A. Adjusting Front Brake . . . 91
   B. Adjusting Rear Brake . . . 91
5. Adjusting Head Lamp Beam . . . 91
6. Tire Pressure . . . 92
7. Adjusting Engine Idling . . . 92
8. Cleaning Air Cleaners . . . 92
9. Changing Gear Box Oil . . . 92
10. Cleaning Muffler Baffle Pipes . . . 93
11. Cleaning Exhaust Pipes . . . 94
12. Drive Chain and Sprocket Maintenance . . . 94
    A. Inspecting Sprockets . . . 94
    B. Installing Sprockets . . . 94
    C. Drive Chain . . . 95
       (1) Adjusting . . . 95
       (2) Maintenance . . . 95
       (3) Tips on Installing Chain Joint Clip . . . 95
13. Adjusting Brake Lamp Switch . . . 95

SUPPLEMENT TO BOOK I (Model T10 and Basic Handbook)

# SPECIFICATIONS OF SUZUKI 250 MODEL T10

| | | |
|---|---|---|
| Dimensions | Overall length | 2,065 mm (81.36 in) |
| | Overall width | 800 mm (31.52 in) |
| | Overall height | 1,050 mm (41.37 in) |
| | Wheelbase | 1,350 mm (53.19 in) |
| | Ground clearance | 135 mm ( 5.32 in) |
| | Seat height | 690 mm (27.19 in) |
| | Tires (front and rear) | 3.00"-17" 4 Ply |
| Weight | Filled weight | 150 kg (330.4 lb) |
| | Distribution | |
| | Front | 68.5 kg (150.9 lb) 45.7% |
| | Rear | 81.5 kg (179.5 lb) 54.3% |
| Performance | Maximum speed | 140 kph (87.5 mph) |
| | Maximum horsepower | 21 hp @ 8,000 rpm |
| | Fuel consumption | 45 km/l @ 40 kph (105 miles/US gal @ 25 mph) |
| | Braking distance | 14 m @ 50 kph (46.7 ft @ 31.2 mph) |
| | Maximum torque | 2.1 kg-m (15.14 ft-lb) @ 7,000 rpm |
| | Climbing ability | 1/3 (18° 25') |
| | Turning radius | 2,000 mm (78.7 in) |
| Engine | Type | air-cooled 2-cycle |
| | Dimensions (L×W×H) | 480×472×348 mm (18.91×18.6×13.71 in) |
| | Cylinders | two, forward inclined |
| | Bore and stroke | 52×58 mm (2.05×2.29 in) |
| | Displacement | 246 cc (15 cu in) |
| | Corrected compression ratio | 6.3:1 |
| | Starting | electric starter (kick also installed) |
| Fuel System | Carburetors | two VM20 |
| | Air cleaners | two resin-processed paper filter |
| | Fuel tank capacity | 10 l (2.64 US gal) including 2 l (0.53 US gal) reserve |
| Lubrication | Crankshaft | gasoline/oil mixture (ratio: 15:1 up to 3,000 km-1,900 miles, 20:1 after that) |
| | Gear box | 500 cc (1.05 US pts) motor oil |
| Ignition System | Spark plugs | two NGK B-7 |
| | Ignition | battery |
| | Ignition timing | 7°~30° BTDC |

| | | |
|---|---|---|
| Electrical Equipment | Generator | directly coupled internal rotating starter dynamo |
| | Battery | 12 V 12 AH |
| | Fuse | 15 A |
| | Head lamp | 12 V 35 W / 35 W |
| | Tail lamp | 12 V 5 W |
| | Brake lamp | 12 V 20 W |
| | Turn signal lamps | 12 V 10 W |
| | Turn signal relay | condenser type |
| | Neutral indicator lamp | 12 V 3 W |
| | Charge indicator lamp | 12 V 3 W |
| | Horn | 1.5 A |
| Transmission | Clutch | wet multi-plate |
| | Gears | 4-speed constant-mesh |
| | Shifting | left foot-operated return change |
| | Gear ratios | Low 2.54 (20.90 total reduction)<br>2nd 1.47 (12.10)<br>3rd 0.96 ( 7.90)<br>Top 0.74 ( 6.10) |
| | Primary reduction ratio | 3.29 |
| | Secondary reduction ratio | 2.50 |
| Suspension System | Front | hyd-aulically damped telescopic fork |
| | Rear | hydraulically damped swinging arm |
| Steering | Angle | 45° (left and right) |
| | Trail | 92 mm (3.62 in) |
| | Caster | 62° |
| Brakes | Front | right hand-operated internal expanding mechanical type |
| | Rear | right foot-operated internal expanding hydraulic type |

# PERFORMANCE CURVES OF T10 ENGINE

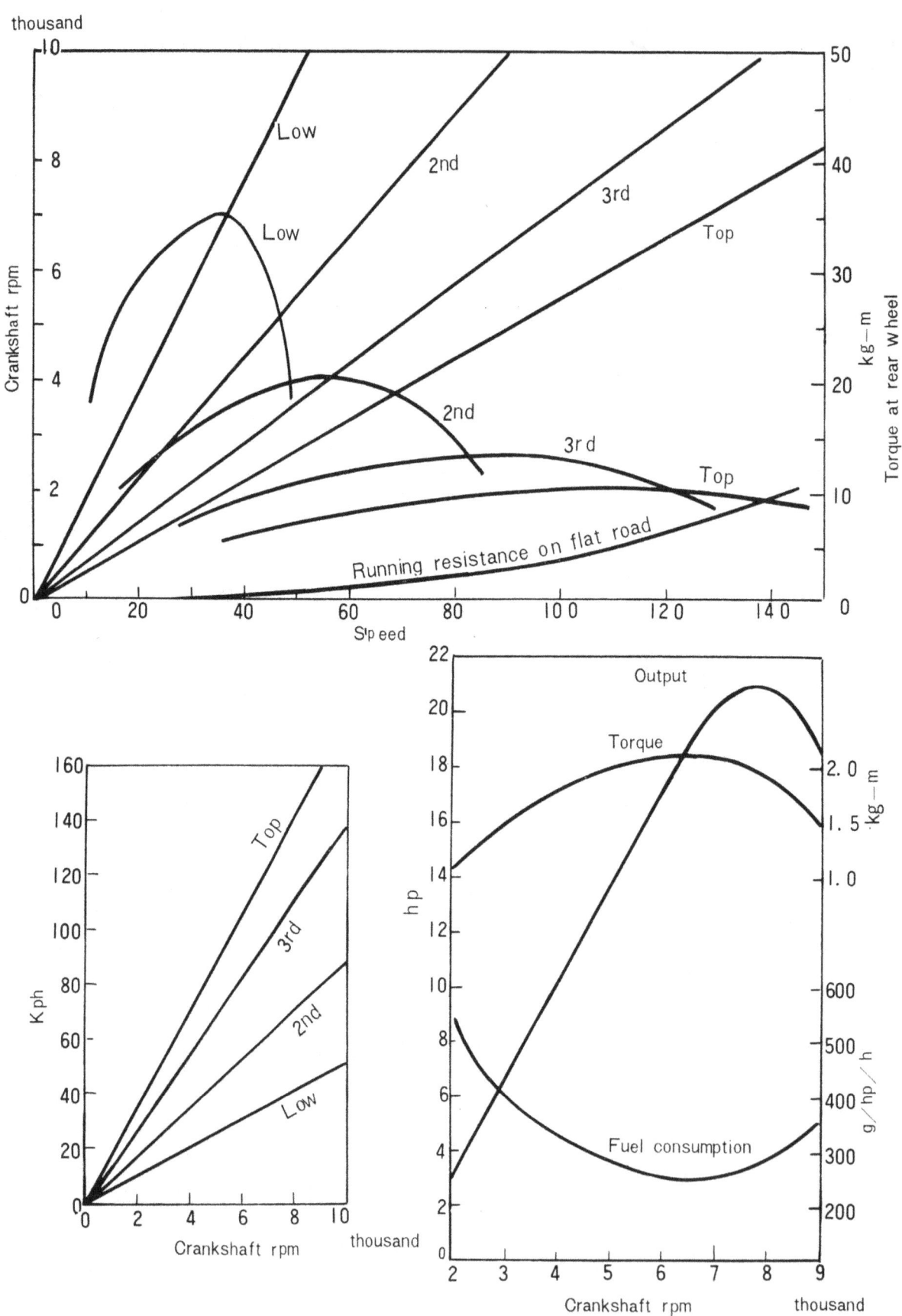

# SPECIAL TOOLS FOR SUZUKI T10

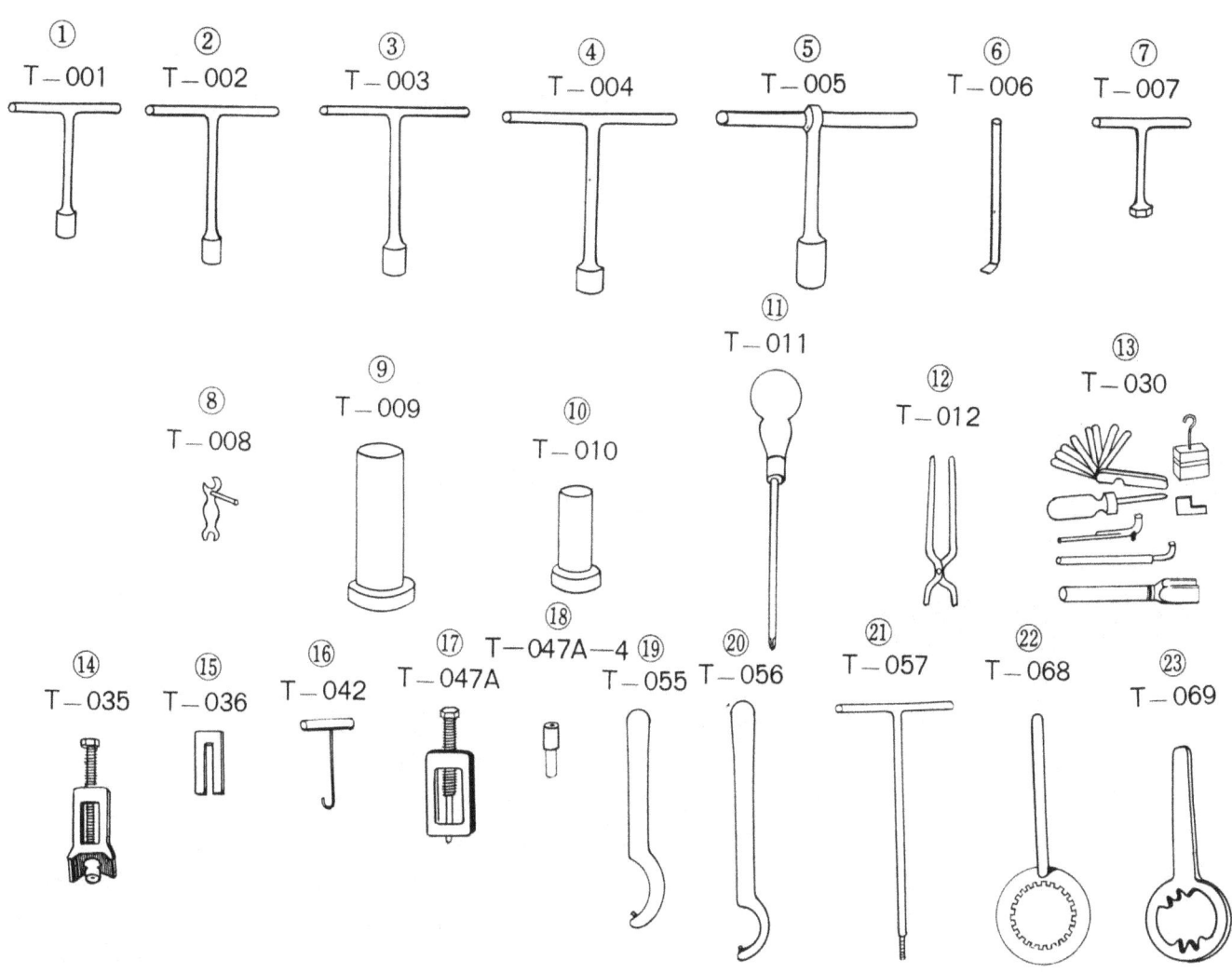

| Ref.No. | Tool No. | Description |
|---|---|---|
| 1 | T-001 | 9 mm socket wrench, for 5 mm nuts, bolts |
| 2 | T-002 | 10 mm socket wrench, for 6 mm nuts, bolts |
| 3 | T-003 | 14 mm socket wrench, for 8 mm nuts, bolts |
| 4 | T-004 | 17 mm socket wrench, for 10 mm nuts, bolts |
| 5 | T-005 | 21 mm socket wrench, for 12 mm nuts, bolts |
| 6 | T-006 | oil seal remover |
| 7 | T-007 | 6 mm stud installing socket wrench |
| 8 | T-008 | contact point wrench, for adjusting points gap, tightening 3mm and 4mm nuts |
| 9 | T-009 | large bearing installing tool, for installing bearings and oil seals |
| 10 | T-010 | small bearing installing tool, for installing bearings and oil seals |
| 11 | T-011 | long phillips screw driver |
| 12 | T-012 | reverse pliers, for removing circlips |

| Ref. No. | Tool No. | Description |
|---|---|---|
| 13 | T-030 | regulator adjusting tool set |
| 14 | T-035 | piston pin remover |
| 15 | T-036 | large piston holder, for holding piston to keep crankshaft from turning |
| 16 | T-042 | clutch spring hook, for removing and installing clutch spring pins |
| 17 | T-047 A | connecting rod bushing tool, for removing and installing small end bushing |
| 18 | T-047 A-4 | connecting rod bushing tool pin |
| 19 | T-055 | large steering stem nut wrench |
| 20 | T-056 | small steering stem nut wrench |
| 21 | T-057 | front fork assembling tool, for pulling up front fork inner tube |
| 22 | T-068 | clutch sleeve hub wrench, for holding clutch sleeve hub when tightening sleeve hub nut |
| 23 | T-069 | engine sprocket wrench, for keeping drive shaft from turning when removing and tightening engine sprocket nut |

# FUEL MIXTURE

The crankshaft, piston and cylinder of a two-cycle engine are lubricated by a small amount of oil mixed with the gasoline burned in the engine, so that such engines require a fuel mixture of gasoline and oil. Use of fuel mixed in the proper ratio of gasoline to oil and use of a good grade of oil and good gasoline is most important for the proper operation and long life of the engine. The fuel mixture ratio for the T10 engine is:

15 : 1 up to 1,000 km (620 miles)
20 : 1 over 1,000 km

For top performance and long life of the engine, the use of a good grade of oil or two-stroke oil is necessary. The following two-stroke oils are recommended: Shell 2T2 Stroke Oil, Shell Outboard Engine Oil, Caltex 2-T Plus Motor Oil, Mobil Mix TT, Mobil Outboard, Esso 2-T Motor Oil.

# TROUBLE SHOOTING

It can be said that the repairs are almost completed once the cause of the trouble is found.

The secret to rapid repairing of the motorcycle is finding the causes of troubles quickly and accurately. The following section pinpoints trouble causes.

### Hard Starting

If the engine does not start even though the choke lever is being used correctly, first check to see if there is fuel in the tank and if the battery is charged.

| Inspection | Checks | Operation |
|---|---|---|
| 1. Fuel supply to carburetor float chamber | If fuel not supplied, check for | clean union bolt, float valve with compressed air or remove carburetor, disassemble and clean |
| | a. clogged fuel line | clean with compressed air |
| | b. clogged fuel cock | disassemble, clean with air |
| | c. clogged, defective float valve | clean with air, or replace |
| | d. clogged fuel tank cap air vent | clean with compressed air |
| 2. Spark. (Remove spark plug, fit in plug cap, hold near cylinder, push starter button and see if spark jumps) | If no spark, check for | |
| | a. defective, dirty plug | clean or replace |
| | b. incorrect plug gap | adjust |
| | c. dirty contact points | clean |
| | d. incorrect contact points gap | adjust |
| | e. defective condenser | replace |
| | f. defective high tension cord | check with tester, replace |
| | g. defective ignition switch | check with tester, replace |
| | h. defective ignition coil | check with tester, replace |
| | i. incorrect ignition timing | check with timing light, adjust |
| 3. Compression | If engine loses compression, check for | |
| | a. worn piston rings, piston, cylinder | replace, rebore |
| | b. damaged cylinder head gasket | replace |
| | c. damaged piston | replace |
| | d. cracked crankcase, scored joining surfaces | repair or replace |
| | e. damaged cylinder base gasket | replace |

When cause is not listed above, start the engine and

| Inspection | Checks | Operation |
|---|---|---|
| 4. See if combustion occurs in engine | If no combustion, check for | |
| | a. too lean fuel | adjust carburetor |
| | b. damaged heat gasket | apply liquid gasket or replace |
| | c. improper ignition timing | adjust |

### Insufficient Motorcycle Speed or Engine Power

First check tire pressure, be sure brakes are not dragging and see that wheels are not dragging due to defective bearings or over-tightened drive chain.

| Inspection | Checks | Operation |
|---|---|---|
| 1. Engine rpm | If engine turns at correct rpm, check for | |
| | slipping clutch (place motorcycle on center stand, engage gears, apply brake. If engine does not stop, clutch is slipping) | adjust clutch or replace cork plates |

| Inspection | Checks | Operation |
|---|---|---|
| | If engine rpm is too low, check for | |
| | a. choked engine | open choke valves |
| | b. dirty air cleaner | clean |
| | c. partially clogged fuel supply system | clean carburetor, fuel line, fuel cock |
| | d. clogged fuel tank cap air vent | clean |
| | e. clogged exhaust pipe, muffler | clean |
| | f. clogged cylinder exhaust port | clean |
| | g. incorrect heat range spark plug | replace with proper plug |
| | h. too rich fuel or too lean fuel | adjust carburetor |
| | i. clogged main jet | clean |
| | j. main jet worked loose | refit |
| | k. incorrect ignition timing | adjust |
| | l. incorrect contact points gap | adjust |
| | m. defective condenser | replace |
| | n. defective ignition coil | replace |
| | o. leaking crankshaft oil seal | replace |
| | p. too tight drive chain | adjust |
| | q. too much play in throttle cable | adjust |

If trouble is not in these parts, run the motorcycle on a paved road and check performance again. If performance is bad.

| Inspection | Checks | Operation |
|---|---|---|
| 2. Engine compression | If compression is below standard 8.0 kg-cm$^2$ (112 psi), check for | |
| | a. piston ring tension too small | replace |
| | b. worn or damaged piston and cylinder | repair or replace |
| | c. damaged cylinder head gasket | replace |
| | d. crankcase leaking compression | repair or replace |
| | e. leaking crankshaft oil seal | replace |
| 3. Carburetor | check for clogging, adjustment | clean, adjust |
| 4. Engine overheating | If engine overheats, check for | |
| | a. carbon accumulated in combustion chamber | remove carbon deposits |
| | b. incorrect fuel mixture | drain fuel tank, replace fuel with correctly mixed fuel |
| | c. slipping clutch | adjust or replace cork plates |
| | d. air inhaled from base gasket, crankcase joining surfaces or crankshaft oil seal | replace damaged gasket and oil seal, apply liquid gasket to joining surfaces, tighten firmly |

## Engine Overheating

If the engine overheats after the breaking in period is finished, check for dragging brake, cylinder fins clogged with mud or too much oil in gear box first.

| Inspection | Checks | Operation |
|---|---|---|
| 1. Engine compression | If engine compression is too high, check for | |
| | a. carbon accumulated in combustion chamber (engine does not stop when ignition switch turned off) | remove carbon deposits |
| | b. too thin cylinder head gasket | replace |
| 2. Exhaust pressure | If exhaust pressure is weak, check for | |
| | a. clogged exhaust pipe | clean |
| | b. dirty baffle pipe | clean |
| | c. clogged cylinder exhaust port | clean |
| | d. clogged muffler | clean |
| 3. Piston ring operation | If piston rings do not operate properly, check for | |
| | carbon in piston ring grooves | clean |
| 4. Too lean fuel/air mixture | If fuel/air mixture supplied by carburetor is too lean, check for | |
| | a. improperly adjusted carburetor | adjust |
| | b. damaged carburetor heat gasket, cylinder base gasket, leaking crankcase joint, leaking crankshaft oil seal | apply liquid gasket to heat gasket, replace base gasket, apply liquid gasket to crankcase joining surfaces and tighten firmly, replace oil seal |
| | c. loose crankshaft oil seal housing | apply liquid gasket |
| 5. Fuel mixture | | mix good grade high octane gasoline and good grade oil, preferably 2-stroke oil, in correct ratio |
| 6. Clutch | | adjust slipping clutch |
| 7. Ignition system | If ignition system does not work properly, check for | |
| | a. defective condenser | check with tester, replace |
| | b. spark plug heat range, worn electrodes | replace with correct plug, adjust gap |
| | c. defective ignition coil | check with tester, replace |
| | d. incorrect ignition timing | adjust |
| | e. defective high tension cord | replace |
| | f. contact breaker points burned, incorrect points gap, defective arm spring, imperfect points contact | polish points, adjust gap, replace points assembly, adjust so points contact evenly and completely |

## Clutch Troubles

| Inspection | Checks | Operation |
|---|---|---|
| 1. Slipping | If clutch slips, check for | |
| | a. worn clutch springs | replace |
| | b. worn or warped pressure plate | repair or replace |
| | c. deformed housing | repair or replace |
| | d. damaged steel plate teeth or hub grooves | replace |
| | e. worn cork plates | replace |
| 2. Dragging | If clutch drags, check for | |
| | a. improper oil viscosity | replace with proper oil |
| | b. defective clutch plate operation | repair or replace |
| | c. unequal clutch spring tension | replace |

## Gear Shifting Troubles

Check to see that clutch works properly and gear box contains proper oil first.

| Inspection | Checks | Operation |
|---|---|---|
| 1. Gear Engagement | If gears do not engage, check for | |
| | a. damaged change cam groove | replace change cam |
| | b. shifter forks not moved smoothly on cam | repair scoring or burrs with emery paper |
| | c. damaged shifter fork | replace |
| | d. seized gears | replace |
| 2. Change Lever | If change lever does not return to normal position, check for | |
| | a. damaged change shaft return spring | replace |
| | b. friction between change shaft and crankcase | repair bent shaft or replace |
| 3. Jumping Out of Gear | If the gears disengage while running, check for | |
| | a. worn or bent shifter fork | replace |
| | b. worn gear dog teeth | replace gear |
| | c. worn or damaged change cam stopper spring | replace spring |

## Engine Noise

Some vibrations and mechanical noise are produced naturally as the internal parts of the engine move at extremely high speeds. If abnormal noise is heard, the cause should be found and repaired.

This calls for rich experience and skill on the part of the mechanic. Abnormal noise can be classified into these three categories; intermittent noise, noise which changes according to operating conditions, and continual noise.

## Intermittent Noise

| Inspection | Checks | Operation |
| --- | --- | --- |
| 1. At abrupt acceleration | If mechanical noise is heard from time to time, check for | |
| | a. excessive piston ring side clearance | replace piston or piston rings |
| | b. piston ring stiffened by carbon deposits | remove carbon deposits |
| | c. excessive clearance between connecting rod small end bushing and piston pin | check small end bushing, piston pin and piston rings and replace if needed |
| | d. excessive clearance in connecting rod big end | repair crankshaft or replace |
| | e. knocking caused by too advanced ignition timing | adjust ignition timing |
| 2. At low rpm | If noise is heard occasionally, check for | |
| | a. excessive clearance between piston and cylinder | install correct size piston or rebore cylinder |
| | b. piston section between ring grooves hitting cylinder (cylinder head vibrates when throttle closed quickly) | repair with emery paper |

## Noise which Changes According to Operating Conditions

| Inspection | Checks | Operation |
| --- | --- | --- |
| 1. When starting engine | If noise is heard only when starting engine, check for | |
| | a. excessive piston clearance (noise stops when engine warms up) | replace piston |
| | b. improperly fitting piston | repair piston section between ring grooves with emery paper |
| 2. At high temperatures | If noise is heard even when engine is hot, check for | |
| | a. excessive piston clearance | replace piston or rebore cylinder |
| | b. bent connecting rod | disassemble crankshaft and repair or replace crankshaft |

## Continual Noise

| Inspection | Checks | Operation |
| --- | --- | --- |
| 1. Crankshaft centering | If flywheel rubs against crankcase, check for | |
| | insufficient clearance between crankshaft and crankcase | use proper shim |

| Inspection | Checks | Operation |
|---|---|---|
| 2. Crankshaft Bearings | If bearings are defective, check for damaged bearing races, rust, damaged steel balls, carbon deposits on bearing | replace bearing |
| 3. Piston Rings | If piston rings are damaged, check for ring catching on port | replace rings |
| 4. Clutch | If clutch noise is heard, check for | |
| | a. excessive clearance between cork plates and clutch housing (noise heard even if clutch disengaged) | replace cork plates |
| | b. excessive clearance between steel plates and hub (noise decreases or ceases when clutch disengaged) | replace steel plates |

## Bad Stability

Check front and rear tire pressure first.

| Inspection | Checks | Operation |
|---|---|---|
| 1. Steering Stem | If handlebar is stiff, check for | |
| | a. excessively tightened steering damper | loosen |
| | b. excessively tightened steering stem nut | loosen |
| | c. damaged steel balls in head bearings | replace balls and races |
| | d. bent steering stem | replace |
| 2. Wheel Alignment | If motorcycle pulls to one side, check for | |
| | a. uneven right and left fork legs | replace fork oil with exactly same amount in each fork leg |
| | b. bent fork inner tube | repair or replace |
| | c. bent swinging arm | repair or replace |
| | d. wheels out of alignment | check to see that they are fitted correctly, align with drive chain adjusters |
| | e. bent or twisted frame | repair or replace |
| 3. Wheel Fitting | If wheel shakes, check for | |
| | a. wheel bearing play | replace bearing |
| | b. deformed rim | replace |
| | c. loose spokes | tighten |
| | d. swinging arm bushing play | replace bushing |
| | e. improperly adjusted drive chain | adjust |
| | f. bent or twisted frame | repair or replace |

## Defective Suspension

Check tire pressure first.

| Inspection | Checks | Operation |
|---|---|---|
| 1. Springs | If damping action is too soft, check for<br>a. worn spring<br>b. oil leak | <br>replace<br>replace front fork oil seal, replace rear shock absorber |
| 2. Fork Inner Tubes | If front fork damping action is too stiff, check for<br>a. excessive oil in forks<br>b. bent inner tube | <br><br>drain and replace with correct amount<br>repair or replace |
| 3. Fork outer tubes | If noise is heard during front fork damping, check for<br>a. oil leak or insufficient oil in fork<br>b. friction between inner tube and slide metal | <br><br>add oil or replace oil seal<br>repair or replace |

## Defective Brakes

Adjust brakes first.

| Inspection | Checks | Operation |
|---|---|---|
| 1. Insufficient Braking | If braking is insufficient, check for<br>a. binding or broken front brake cable<br>b. air in hydraulic brake system<br>c. damaged brake hose<br>d. loose hydraulic brake system connections<br>e. defective contact between brake linings and drum<br>f. dirt, water or brake oil in drum<br>g. oil or grease impregnated brake linings | <br>lubricate cable or replace<br>bleed out air<br>replace<br>tighten<br><br>repair or replace brake shoes<br><br>clean drum, replace rear brake cylinder oil seals<br>clean or replace brake shoes |
| 2. Abnormal Noise when Braking | If abnormal noise is heard when brakes are applied, check for<br>a. worn brake linings<br>b. foreign particles on brake linings<br>c. rough brake drum internal surface<br>d. insufficiently lubricated brake cam | <br><br>replace<br>clean linings<br>repair<br><br>grease |

| Inspection | Checks | Operation |
|---|---|---|
| 3. Brake Cannot Be Adjusted | If the brake cannot be adjusted with brake adjuster, check for | |
| | a. worn brake linings | replace |
| | b. worn brake cam | replace |

## Insufficient Battery Charging

If the battery discharges or charge indicator lamp does not turn off even when the engine rpm is high, check the electrical system with a voltage meter without the battery installed.

| Inspection | Checks | Operation |
|---|---|---|
| 1. Wiring | If wiring circuit is defective, check for | |
| | a. defective connections | reconnect and tighten |
| | b. damaged wiring harness cover | repair with vinyl tape or replace |
| | c. damaged wire ends | tighten terminals firmly |
| 2. Dynamo | If dynamo is defective, check for | |
| | a. dirty or burned commutator | wash dirty commutator with fresh gasoline, polish burned commutator with emery paper, check carbon brushes and brush springs |
| | b. defective armature (ground regulator F terminal, remove D terminal and connect to voltmeter. If generating voltage without load is below 13.5 volts at 1,550 rpm, armature is defective) If circuit is formed between commutater segments and core, armature is defective. | replace |
| | c. defective stator (if terminal D to terminal F circuit does not conduct electricity, stator is defective. If terminal D to yoke circuit conducts electric current, stator is defective) | replace<br><br>repair insulation or replace stator |
| | d. worn or damaged carbon brushes | replace |
| | e. defective regulator | adjust or replace |

## Starter Troubles

Charge the battery fully.

| Inspection | Checks | Operation |
|---|---|---|
| 1. Noise when Button Pushed | If a click is not heard when starter button is pushed, check for | |
| | a. damaged fuse | replace |

| Inspection | Checks | Operation |
|---|---|---|
| | b. damaged or loose starter switch circuit (yellow cord with green tracer) | repair |
| | c. damaged starter switch relay coil | replace regulator |
| 2. Switching Sound Heard But Starter Does Not Turn | If a switching sound is heard when the button is pushed but the starter does not turn and neutral indicator lamp is on, check for<br>a. loose starter switch connections<br>b. improper carbon brush contact or brushes pulled up | <br><br><br><br>tighten regulator B.M terminals<br>fit properly or replace weak brush spring |
| | If neutral indicator lamp is extremely dim, check for<br>a. loose battery terminal connection<br>b. armature layer short or circuit between battery, starter switch relay and starter dynamo grounded | <br><br>tighten<br>repair wiring harness and replace armature or regulator if needed |
| 3. Starter Turns Slowly When Cold | If starter turns at less than 100 rpm when temperature is below −5°C (24°F), check for<br>a. gear box oil viscosity<br>b. lowered battery performance due to low temperature | <br><br><br>replace with proper oil<br>use kick starter |
| 4. Starter Turns Slowly at Normal Temperature | If starter turns at less than 100 rpm at normal temperatures, check for<br>a. seized engine<br>b. friction between armature core and stator | <br><br>repair<br>file armature core |

Most troubles in the electrical system are caused by the owner's misuse of the motorcycle. The T10 is designed to give excellent performance at all speeds, but the electrical equipment works best if engine is operated at 1,550 rpm (28 kph, 17 mph in top gear) or faster at all times. When riding slower than this speed, use a lower gear to keep the battery from discharging.

# ENGINE

## 1. Removing Engine From Frame

| Operation | Tools |
|---|---|
| Remove wiring from engine | screw driver |
| Close fuel cock | |
| Remove oil plug and drain oil from gearbox | 21 mm socket wrench |
| Remove footrest rubber | 14 mm open end wrench |
| Remove change lever | 10 mm open end wrench |
| Remove engine sprocket cover and dynamo inspection cap | long phillips screw driver |
| Take drive chain off of engine sprocket (clip chain joint back on end of chain) | pliers, small screw driver |
| Remove choke lever | screw driver |
| Remove right and left carburetor covers | large phillips screw driver |
| Remove from carburetors: | |
|     Right and left fuel lines | 12mm open end wrench |
|     Right and left throttle valves | |
|     Right and left air cleaner tube clamps | phillips screw driver |
| Remove right and left spark plug caps | |
| Remove two short cylinder supporting bolts | 14 mm socket wrench |
| Remove kick starter lever | 12 mm open end wrench |
| Remove right and left exhaust pipes and mufflers | 10 mm socket wrench |
| Remove 3 engine fitting bolts | 17, 14 and 12 mm socket wrenches |

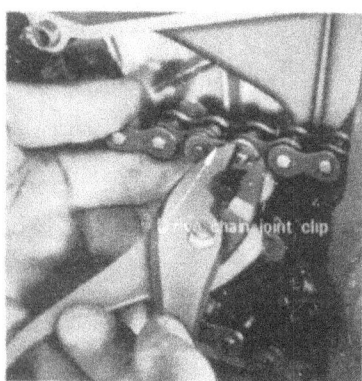

Fig. 1
CUTTING CHAIN JOINT

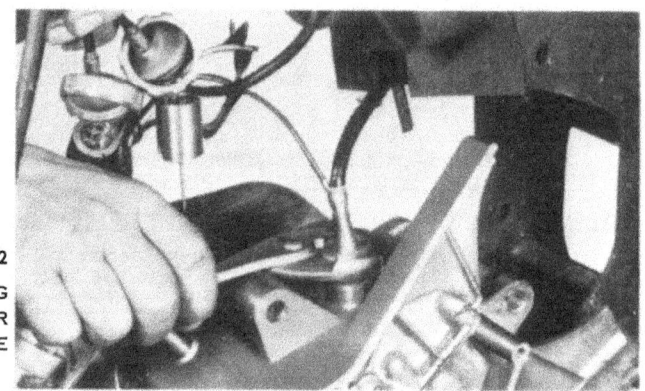

Fig. 2
DISCONNECTING SPEEDOMETER CABLE

Fig. 3
VIEW OF MACHINE AFTER ENGINE HAS BEEN REMOVED

Fig. 4
ENGINE REMOVED FROM FRAME

The engine can be removed from the frame. The speedometer cable must be removed from the engine with pliers as the engine is being taken from the frame. See Fig. 2. The engine after removed from the frame is shown in Fig. 4.

# 2. Disassembly

## A. Work which Can Be Done with Engine in Frame

- Removing spark plugs.
- Removing cylinder heads.
- Removing cylinders.
- Removing piston rings.
- Removing pistons.
- Removing piston pins.
- Removing connecting rod small end bushings.
- Changing gear box oil.
- Removing primary gear.
- Removing primary pinion.
- Repairing clutch.
- Removing change shaft.
- Removing engine sprocket.
- Adjusting contact points.
- Adjusting ignition timing.
- Replacing carbon brushes in starter dynamo.
- Removing carburetors.
- Removing air cleaners.
- Removing mufflers and exhaust pipes.

## B. Work for which Engine Must Be Removed from Frame

- Removing crankshaft.
- Removing transmission shafts.
- Removing kick starter gears.
- Removing change system (except shaft).
- Removing speedometer drive gears.

## C. Disassembling

| Operation | Part No. | Part Name | Q'ty | Tools | Remarks |
|---|---|---|---|---|---|
| Removing Carburetors | T 10-1631 K 1 | right carburetor assy | 1 | | |
| | T 10-1632 K 1 | left carburetor assy | 1 | | |
| | S H 1631 K 1-57 | outlet clamp | 2 | | |
| | S H 1631 K 1-16 | outlet clamp bolt | 2 | large screw driver | |
| | S H 1631 K 1-55 | outlet clamp nut | 2 | | |
| | S H 1631 K 1-56 | outlet clamp wasther | 2 | | |

**Fig. 5**
ORDER OF LOOSENING CYLINDER HEAD BOLTS

**Fig. 6**
SLIPPING CYLINDER OFF PISTON

| Operation | Part No. | Part Name | Q'ty | Tools | Remarks |
|---|---|---|---|---|---|
| Removing Cylinder Heads | S B 3210 | spark plug | 2 | 21 mm socket wrench | |
| | T 10-1111 | right cylinder head | 1 | | |
| | T 10-1112 | left cylinder head | 1 | | |
| | T A 1122 | cylinder head bolt | 8 | 14 mm socket wrench | not in sequence |
| | WM 081 | cylinder head washer | 8 | | 8 mm |
| | T 10-1121 | cylinder head gasket | 2 | | |
| Removing Cylinders | N K 081 | cylinder fitting nut | 8 | 12 mm open end wrench | 8 mm |
| | W S 08 | lock washer | 8 | | 8 mm |
| | T 10-1211 | right cylinder | 1 | | |
| | T 10-1212 | left cylinder | 1 | | |
| | T A 1221 | cylinder gasket | 2 | | |
| | A A E 3121 | piston ring (top) | 2 | | chrome plated |
| | A A E 3122 | piston ring (second) | 2 | | parkerized |
| Disassembling Starter Dynamo | T B 3193 K 1 | armature bolt | 1 | large piston holder 14 mm socket wrench | place piston holder under piston on dynamo side |
| | W S 08 | lock washer | 1 | | 8 mm |
| | T B 3113 K 1 | timing advancer assy | 1 | | |
| | S C 3191 K 1 | stator fitting screw | 3 | large phillips screw driver | |
| | W S 06 | lock washer | 3 | | 6 mm |
| | T B 7420-9 | indicator lamp positive wire | 1 | small phillips screw driver | remove from neutral indicator switch |
| | S B 3111 K 1-31 | carbon brush | 4 | clutch spring hook | pull away from commutator (See Fig. 8) |
| | T B 3111 K 1 | stator assy | 1 | | |
| | T B 3112 K 1 | armature | 1 | armature remover 14 mm socket wrench, large piston holder | |

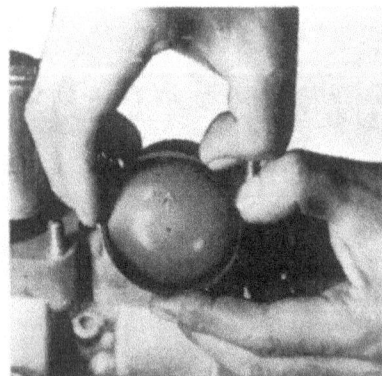

Fig. 7
REMOVING PISTON RING

Fig. 8
PULLING UP CARBON BRUSH SPRING

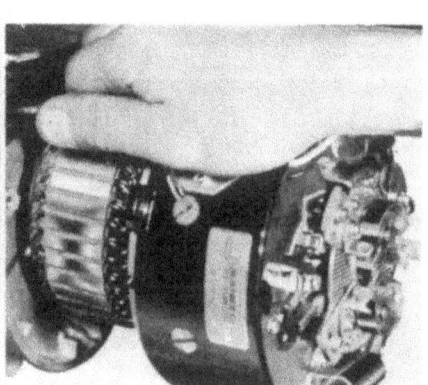

Fig. 9
REMOVING STATOR FROM CRANKCASE

| Operation | Part No. | Part Name | Q'ty | Tools | Remarks |
|---|---|---|---|---|---|
| Removing Neutral Switch | D N 0515 | neutral indicator switch fitting screw | 3 | large phillips screw driver | |
| | S B 3411A | neutral indicator switch | 1 | | |
| | S B 3412A | neutral indicator switch gasket | 1 | | |
| | S B 3414 | neutral indicator switch ball | 1 | | |
| | S B 3415 | neutral indicator switch ball spring | 1 | | |
| Removing Engine Sprocket | S H 2312 | clutch push rod | 1 | | |
| | S B 2591 | engine sprocket nut | 1 | 33 mm open end wrench | |
| | S B 2592 | engine sprocket washer | 1 | hammer, chisel | straighten with chisel |
| | T 10-5211 | engine sprocket | 1 | engine sprocket wrench | 12 teeth |
| | T A 2512 | engine sprocket spacer | 1 | | |
| Removing Crankcase Right Cover | P N N 0665 | fitting screw | 6 | large phillips screw driver | 6x65 mm |
| | P N N 0635 | fitting screw | 1 | large phillips screw driver | 6x35 mm |
| | P N S 0630 | fitting screw | 1 | large phillips screw driver | 6x30 mm |
| | T A 1521 | crankcase right cover | 1 | rubber hammer | strike solid part lightly |
| | T A 1531A | crankcase right cover gasket | 1 | | |
| Disassembling Clutch | A A M 2172 | clutch spring pin | 6 | clutch spring hook | |
| | T 10-2244 | clutch pressure plate | 1 | | |
| | T 10-2241 | clutch cork plate | 5 | | |
| | T 10-2242 | clutch steel plate | 5 | | |
| | S K 2311 | clutch release rod | 1 | | |
| | S G 2591 | engine sprocket nut | 1 | clutch sleeve hub wrench, 29 mm socket wrench | insert piston holder |
| | S H 2292 | clutch sleeve hub washer | 1 | chisel, hammer | straighten with chisel |
| | T 10-2231 | clutch sleeve hub | 1 | clutch sleeve hub wrench | |

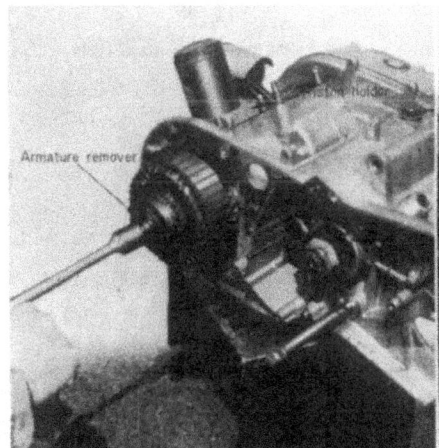

Fig. 10
REMOVING ARMATURE

Fig. 11
NEUTRAL INDICATOR SWITCH

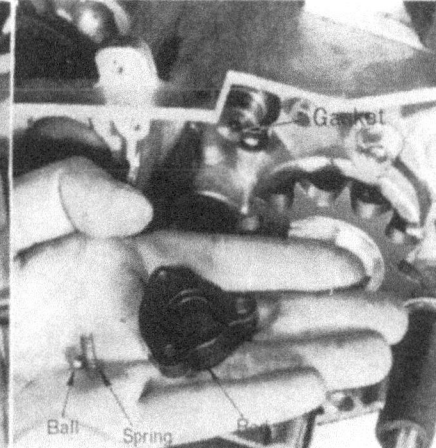

Fig. 12
DISASSEMBLED NEUTRAL INDICATOR SWITCH

| Operation | Part No. | Part Name | Q'ty | Tools | Remarks |
|---|---|---|---|---|---|
| | S B 2222 | clutch housing thrust washer | 1 | | |
| | T 10-2210 | clutch housing comp | 1 | | |
| | T 10-2221 | clutch housing spacer | 1 | | |
| | S B 2222 | clutch housing thrust washer | 1 | | |
| Removing Primary Pinion | S B 2591 | engine sprocket nut | 1 | piston holder, 33mm open end wrench | |
| | T A 2192 | primary pinion washer | 1 | chisel, hammer | straighten with chisel |
| | T 10-2111 | primary pinion | 1 | large screw driver | |
| | K W 043 | key | 1 | hammer, chisel | 4 mm thick |
| | T 10-2112 | primary pinion spacer | 1 | | |
| Removing Kick Starter Shaft Return Spring | S K 2754 | kick starter shaft return spring guide | 1 | pliers | |
| | S K 2741 | kick starter shaft return spring | 1 | pliers | |
| Removing Change Shaft | S B 2666 | change shaft thrust washer circlip | 1 | screw driver | |
| | S B 2665 | change shaft thrust washer | 1 | | |
| | C S 12 | circlip | 1 | reverse pliers | |
| | T A 2661 | change shaft comp | 1 | | |
| Removing Drive Shaft Oil Reservoir Cap | P S 0512 | fitting screw | 2 | phillips screw driver | 5×12 mm |
| | T A 2492 | drive shaft oil reservoir cap | 1 | | |

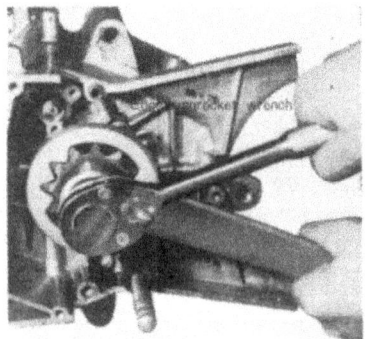

Fig. 13
LOOSENING ENGINE SPROCKET NUT

Fig. 14
SPLITTING CRANKCASE RIGHT COVER

Fig. 15
DISASSEMBLING CLUTCH

Fig. 16
LOOSENING CLUTCH SLEEVE HUB NUT

Fig. 17
LOOSENING PRIMARY PINION NUT

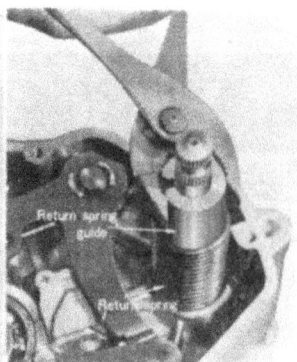

Fig. 18
REMOVING KICK STARTER SHAFT RETURN SPRING GUIDE

| Operation | Part No. | Part Name | Q'ty | Tools | Remarks |
|---|---|---|---|---|---|
| Separating Crankcases | BGS 08105 | crankcase bolt | 2 | 14 mm socket wrench | 8×105 mm |
| | BGS 0895 | crankcase bolt | 2 | 14 mm socket wrench | 8×95 mm |
| | BGS 0880 | crankcase bolt | 2 | 14 mm socket wrench | 8×80 mm |
| | WK 08 | small flat washer | 6 | | 8 mm |
| | WS 08 | lock washer | 6 | | 8 mm |
| | BGS 06100 | crankcase bolt | 2 | 10 mm socket wrench | 6×100 mm |
| | BGS 0680 | crankcase bolt | 2 | 10 mm socket wrench | 6×80 mm |
| | BGS 0665 | crankcase bolt | 1 | 10 mm socket wrench | 6×65 mm |
| | BGS 0660 | crankcase bolt | 2 | 10 mm socket wrench | 6×60 mm |
| | BGS 0655 | crankcase bolt | 2 | 10 mm socket wrench | 6×55 mm |
| | WM 061 | flat washer | 9 | | 6 mm |
| | WS 06 | lock washer | 9 | | 6 mm |
| | TA 1510A | crankcase assy | 1 | rubber hammer | |

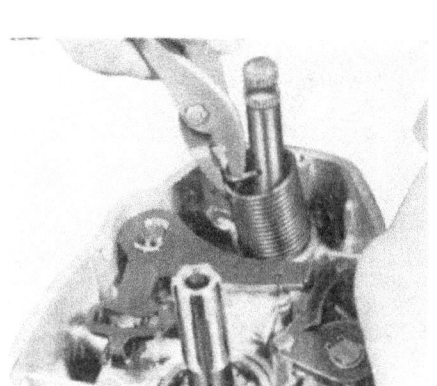

Fig. 19
REMOVING KICK STARTER SHAFT RETURN SPRING

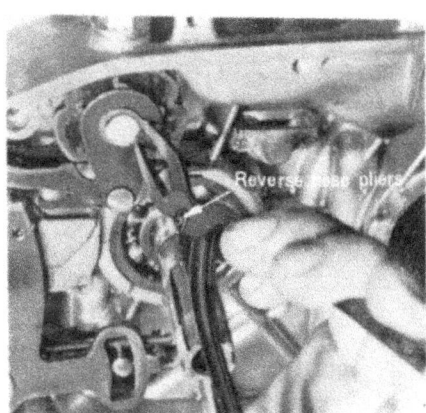

Fig. 20
REMOVING SHIFTING CAM PIN FITTING PLATE CIRCLIP

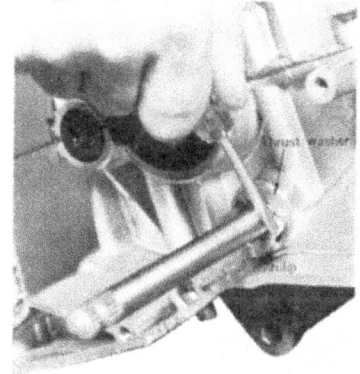

Fig. 21-1
REMOVING CHANGE SHAFT THRUST WASHER CIRCLIP

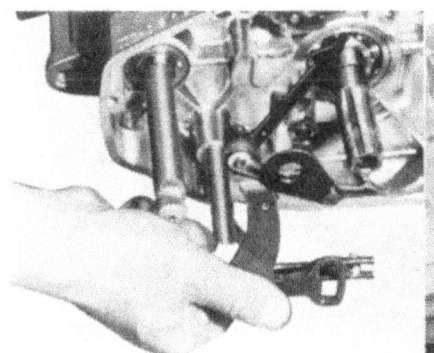

Fig. 21-2
REMOVING CHANGE SHAFT

Fig. 22
REMOVING DRIVE SHAFT OIL RESERVOIR

Fig. 23
SPLITTING CRANKCASES

NOTE: Turn the engine upside down with the upper case on the bottom and strike a thick part of the lower case gently with a rubber hammer to separate the cases.

CAUTION: Do not strike a thin section of the lower case with the hammer. Do not try to pry the cases apart with a screw driver or similar tool, as this will damage the joining surfaces.

When the cases are separated about 10 mm (1/2 inch), check to see that the crankshaft and gear assembly is in the upper case (which is on the bottom). If they are remaining in the lower c se, shake the assembly or strike the ends of the shafts gently with a rubber hammer until they fall into the upper case.

| Operation | Part No. | Part Name | Q'ty | Tools | Remarks |
|---|---|---|---|---|---|
| Disassembling Countershaft | T 10-2312 | clutch inner push rod | 1 | | |
| | S B 2371 | push rod oil seal | 1 | | |
| | T A 2481 A | countershaft bushing | 1 | | |
| | T A 2451 | top pinion thrust washer | 1 | | |
| | S G 2465 | top pinion adjusting washer | 0 ~ 2 | | 0.2 mm thick |
| | S G 2465 T 01 | top pinion adjusting washer | 0 ~ 2 | | 0.3 mm thick |
| | T A 2424 | top pinion comp | 1 | | |
| | T A 2451 | top pinion thrust washer | 1 | | |
| | T A 2422 | second pinion | 1 | | |
| | T A 2462 | transmission shaft circlip | 1 | reverse pliers | |
| | S B 2461 | third pinion thrust washer | 1 | | |
| | T 10-2423 | third pinion | 1 | | |
| | J K 6304N S | slotted ball bearing | 1 | bearing puller | |
| Disassembling Drive Shaft | T A 2482 A | drive shaft bushing | 1 | | |
| | T A 2451 | top pinion thrust washer | 1 | | |
| | S G 2465 | top pinion adjusting washer | 0 ~ 2 | | 0.2 mm thick |
| | S G 2465 T 01 | top pinion adjusting washer | 0 ~ 2 | | 0.3 mm thick |
| | T A 2441 A | low gear comp | 1 | | |
| | T A 2451 | top pinion thrust washer | 1 | | |
| | T 10-2443 | third gear | 1 | | |
| | T A 2462 | transmission shaft circlip | 1 | reverse pliers | |
| | S B 2461 | second gear thrust washer | 1 | | |
| | T A 2442 | second gear | 1 | | |
| | S G 2463 | adjusting washer | 0 ~ 1 | | 0.2 mm(0.008in) thick |
| | S G 2463 S 0.3 | adjusting washer | 0 ~ 1 | | 0.3 mm (0.01 in) thick |
| | T A 2471 | drive shaft oil seal | 1 | | |
| | J K 6304N S | slotted ball bearing | 1 | bearing puller | |

| Operation | Part No. | Part Name | Q'ty | Tools | Remarks |
|---|---|---|---|---|---|
| Disassembling Kick Starter Shaft | S K 2753 | kick starter shaft left bushing | 1 | | |
| | S K 2787 | kiak starter pinion outer thrust washer | 2 | | one on each side of adjusting washer SK 2786 |
| | S K 2786 | kick starter pinion adjusting washer | 1 | | |
| | S K 2721 | kick starter pinion | 1 | | 24 teeth |
| | S K 2785 | kick starter pinion inner thrust washer | 1 | | |
| | S K 2711 | kick starter pawl | 1 | | |
| | T A 2712 | kick starter shaft pawl roller | 1 | | |
| | T A 2713 | kick starter shaft pawl spring | 1 | | |
| | C S 20 | kick starter shaft circlip | 1 | reverse pliers | |
| | S K 2781 | kick starter shaft thrust washer | 1 | | |
| | S K 2752 | kick starter shaft right bushing | 1 | | |
| | S K 2781 | kick starter shaft thrust washer | 1 | | |
| Disassembling Speedometer Drive System | T A 2914 | speedometer pinion circlip | 1 | small screw driver | |
| | T A 2913 | speedometer pinion thrust washer | 1 | | |
| | T 10-2912 A | speedometer pinion | 1 | | |
| | T A 2913 | speedometer pinion thrust washer | 1 | | |
| | N K 081 | small hexagon nut | 1 | 12 mm open end wrench | 8 mm |
| | W S.08 | lock washer | 1 | | 8 mm |
| | W K 08 | small flat washer | 1 | | 8 mm |
| | T A 2911 | speedometer pinion shaft | 1 | | |
| | N G 051 | hexagon nut | 1 | 9 mm socket wrench | 5 mm |
| | T A 2926 | speedometer gear lock washer | 1 | chisel, hammer | straighten with chisel |
| | T 10-2921 | speedometer gear | 1 | | |
| | T A 2925 | speedometer gear thrust washer | 1 | | |

Fig. 24
GEARING & CRANKSHAFT

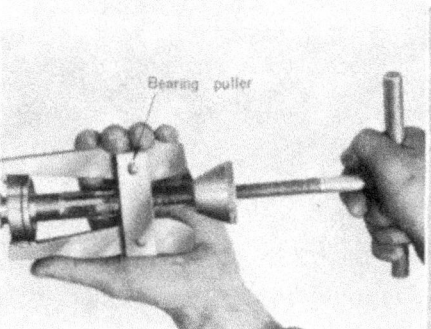

Fig. 25
EXTRACTING COUNTER-SHAFT BEARING

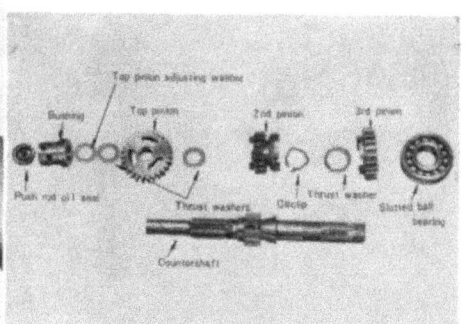

Fig. 26
DISASSEMBLED COUNTER-SHAFT

| Operation | Part No. | Part Name | Q'ty | Tools | Remarks |
|---|---|---|---|---|---|
| | T A 2922 A | speedometer gear shaft | 1 | | |
| | T A 2925 | speedometer gear thrust washer | 1 | | strike from inside toward outside |
| | T A 2923 | speedometer gear bushing | 1 | plastic hammer | |
| Disassembling Shifting Cam | S B 2642 | shifting cam stopper holder | 1 | 14 mm socket wrench | |
| | S B 2645 | shifting cam stopper adjusting washer | 0~2 | | 0.5 mm thick |
| | T A 2636 | shifting cam guide washer | 1 | chisel, hammer | straighten with chisel |
| | S B 2643 | shifting cam stopper spring | 1 | | |
| | S B 2641 | shifting cam stopper | 1 | | |
| | T A 2635 | shifting cam guide | 1 | 17 mm socket wrench | |
| | T A 2634 | shifting cam guide roller | 1 | | |
| | P W 2525 | cotter pin | 2 | thin nose pliers | 2.5×25 mm |
| | S K 2621 | gear shifting fork guide | 2 | | |
| | S K 2622 | gear shifting fork guide roller | 2 | | |
| | T 10-2631 | shifting cam | 1 | | |
| | T 10-2611 | gear shifting fork | 2 | | |

CAUTION: When disassembling the shifting cam, be careful not to scratch or damage the upper and lower case joining surfaces. They should be covered with a clean rag to prevent damage.

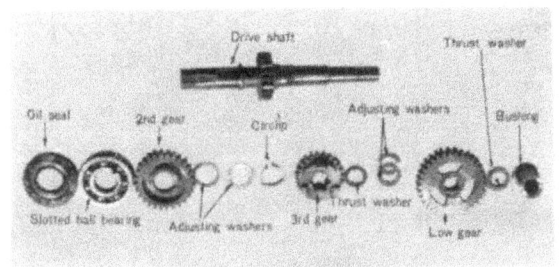

Fig. 27
DISASSEMBLED DRIVE SHAFT

Fig. 28
DISASSEMBLED KICK STARTER SHAFT

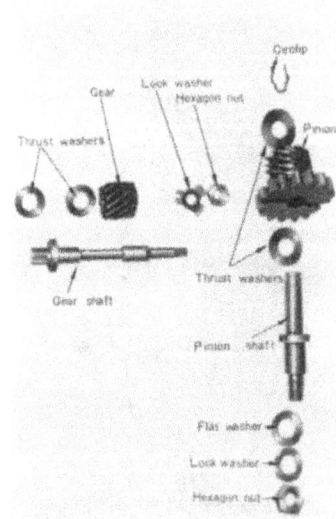

Fig. 29
DISASSEMBLED SPEEDOMETER DRIVE SYSTEM

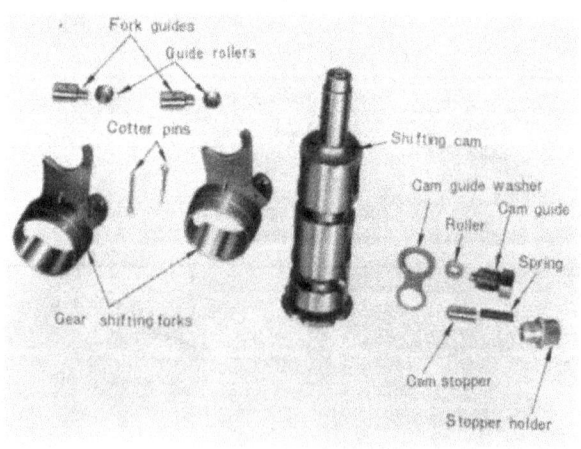

Fig. 30
DISASSEMBLED SHIFTING CAM & FORKS

# 3. Assembling

## A. Engine Assembling Tips

The engine is the heart of the motorcycle and consists of precisely manufactured parts, which must be handled and assembled most carefully.

When working on the engine, keep your hands and tools clean at all times.

## B. Tools, etc.

Before beginning work, prepare work benches, necessary tools, clean rags and cleaning solvent for washing parts.

Fig. 31
DISASSEMBLED ENGINE ON WORK BENCHES

## C. Tips on Tightening Nuts and Bolts

Tighten nuts and bolts in accordance with standard torque recommendations. See illustrations.

Fit the piston holder under the piston skirt when tightening parts where the crankshaft needs to be kept from turning. Do not allow the engine sprocket wrench and clutch sleeve hub holder to be supported by the shaft or crankcase.

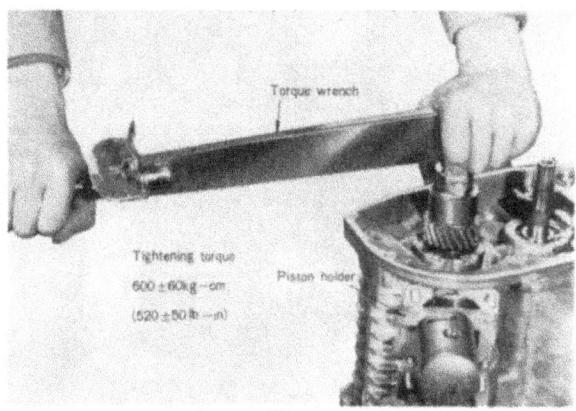

Fig. 32
TIGHTENING PRIMARY PINION NUT

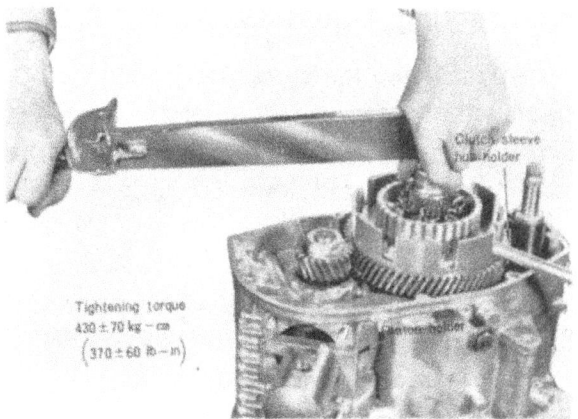

Fig. 33
TIGHTENING CLUTCH SLEEVE HUB NUT

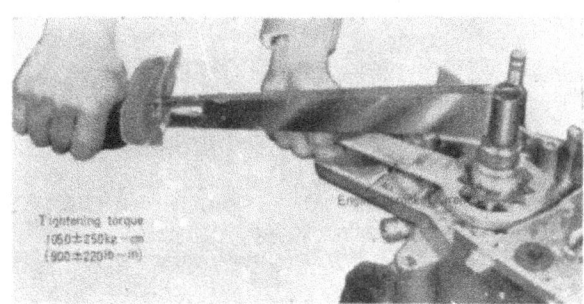

Fig. 34
TIGHTENING ENGINE SPROCKET NUT

Fig. 35
TIGHTENING ARMATURE BOLT

## D. Assembling Procedure

The engine can be assembled in the reverse order of the disassembly procedure listed in the previous section. Before assembling the engine, wash all parts except the dynamo with solvent. Wipe the dynamo with a clean rag.

After washing the parts, place them on a dry clean rag so that the cleaning solvent will be absorbed from them.

## E. Applying Liquid Gasket

After wiping the crankcase joining surfaces clean with a rag, apply a small amount of Suzuki Sildar (TE-1611) two or three times to upper crankcase and lower crankcase joining surfaces.

When installing the parts in the crankcase, be sure to fit them into the upper crankcase. Fit the lower crankcase after the crankshaft and transmission are installed.

Fig. 36
APPLYING SUZUKI SILDAR TO CRANKCASE JOINING SURFACES

## F. Installing Transmission Gears

The gear shifting forks are interchangeable, but the convex part must be aligned with the concave part of the cam. See Fig. 37.

Insert the shifting cam guide cotter pins from the inside of the gear shifting forks and spread both ends of the pins. Always use new cotter pins when reassembling the shifting mechanism. After fitting the shifting cam guide and shifting cam stopper holder, test the shifting cam to see that it works correctly. See Fig. 39. Turning the shifting cam with a 10 mm wrench,

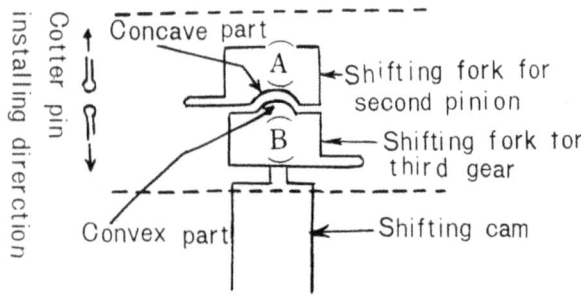

Fig. 37
INSTALLING SHIFTING FORKS

Fig. 38    DISASSEMBLED SHIFTING CAM

Fig. 39    TESTING SHIFTER FORK OPERATION ON SHIFTING CAM

check to see that the gear shifting forks move smoothly on the cam in both directions. There should not be any play in the thrust direction.

The transmission of the T10 motorcycle is a return type, so that the cam does not turn completely around. After testing, shift the cam into the neutral position.

## G. Speedometer Drive Gear

After assembling the speedometer pinion and speedometer gear, turn the speedometer pinion with your fingers to see that the pinion turns smoothly. See Fig. 36. It can be adjusted by using thrust washers on the speedometer gear shaft. See Fig. 29.

Fig. 40
TESTING SPEEDOMETER DRIVE OPERATION

## H. Dowel Pins, Slotted Bearing and Crankshaft Oil Seal Positioning Pieces

Install the proper dowel pins and slotted bearing positioning pieces when assembling the crankshaft and transmission gears. See Fig. 41.

Dowel pins A, B and C shown in the illustration are interchangeable, but D and E have larger diameters. Dowel pin D located on the outer side of the case is longer than dowel pin E on the inner side. Slotted bearing positioning pieces 2, 3 and 4 are interchangeable, but positioning piece 1 is thinner than these.

Fig. 42
BRINGING OIL SEALS TO INSIDE

Fig. 41
DOWEL PINS & POSITIONING PIECES

## I. Installing Crankshaft Assembly

Take care not to damage the pistons when installing the crankshaft assembly. Strike the assembly gently with a plastic hammer if necessary to fit the crankshaft into the correct position in the crankcase. Push the right and left crankshaft oil seals toward the center of the crankshaft when installing them. See Fig. 42.

## J. Tips on Installing Countershaft and Drive Shaft

When installing the countershaft and drive shaft in the crankcase, fit the countershaft second pinion and drive shaft third gear on the shafts with the gear facing the bushing side as shown in Fig. 43. Guiding the second

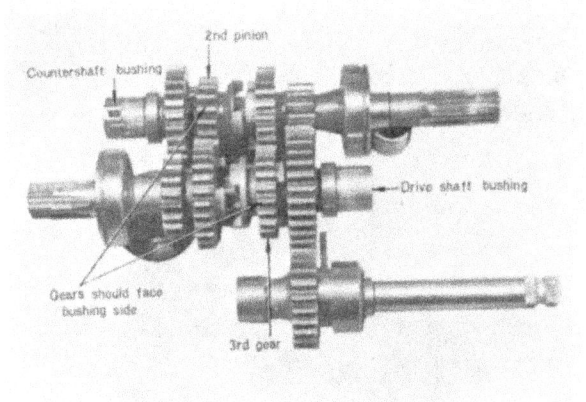

Fig. 43
TRANSMISSION GEAR ENGAGEMENTS

pinion and third gear with the gear shifting forks, fix the shafts on dowel pins and positioning pieces. Gently strike bearings and bushings with a plastic hammer if necessary to make them fit properly.

The bushings for the countershaft and drive shaft have the same inside diameter, but the countershaft bushing has an oil groove and the drive shaft bushing does not. Do not fit them incorrectly. See Fig. 44.

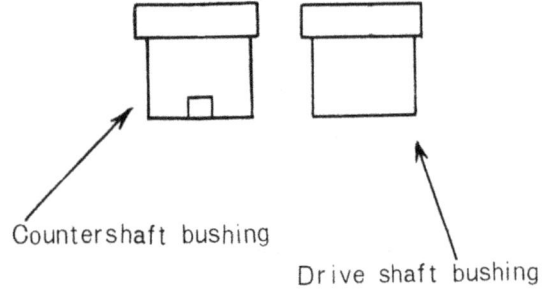

Fig. 44
COUNTERSHAFT BUSHING
& DRIVE SHAFT BUSHING

Push the oil seals to the inside of the case. Apply oil generously to gears, bearings, shifting forks, shafts, bushings and all rubbing parts of the crankshaft and transmission. Turn all the shafts by hand and lubricate all parts thoroughly, at the same time checking to make sure that the gears and shafts turn smoothly before installing.

## K. Testing Transmission Gears

Use a 10 mm wrench on the shifting cam pin retainer bolt to turn the cam and check to see that gears shift smoothly and gear engagements are smooth at all speeds. See Fig. 45.

Fig. 45
TESTING GEAR SHIFTING
SYSTEM OPERATION

## L. Tips on Fitting Lower Crankcase

Place the kick starter shaft with the finger on the large section down so it does not hit the lower case. See Fig. 46.

Fig. 46
INSTALLING KICK STARTER SHAFT

Be sure the gears are in the neutral position.

Fit the lower crankcase gently. Strike the thick part of the crankcase gently with a rubber hammer to make it fit firmly, if necessary.

After fitting the lower crankcase, check to see that the shafts turn smoothly and that the oil seals are fitted properly.

## M. Tightening Crankcase Bolts

Lightly tighten crankcase bolts with a socket wrench, following the tightening sequence shown by the numbers marked on the lower crankcase, and then tighten the bolts with a torque wrench. See Fig. 47. Proper tightening torque of 6 mm bolts is 100 kg-cm (85 lb-in) and of 8 mm bolts is 200 kg-cm (170 lb-in).

Fig. 47
TIGHTENING CRANKCASE JOINING BOLTS

## N. Installing Oil Reservoir Caps, Change Lever, Kick Starter Parts

Install oil reservoir caps as shown in Fig. 48.

**Fig. 48**
FITTING DRIVE SHAFT RESERVOIR CAP

Fit the change lever on the change shaft and test the operation of the gear shifting system. Do not use pliers or similar tools to turn the change shaft. See Fig. 49

**Fig. 49**
TESTING GEAR SHIFTING
SYSTEM OPERATION

Install the kick starter shaft return spring. See Fig. 50. Install the kick starter shaft return spring guide. See Fig. 51.

**Fig. 50**
INSTALLING KICK STARTER SHAFT RETURN SPRING

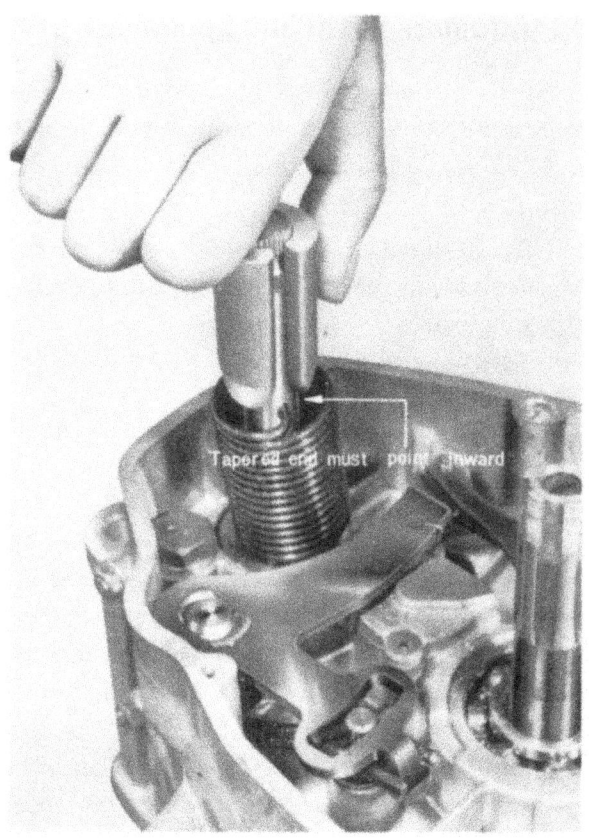

**Fig. 51**
INSTALLING KICK STARTER
SHAFT RETURN SPRING GUIDE

## O. Installing Clutch Push Rods

Install the long clutch push rod into the countershaft from the hub side and then insert the short inner push rod flat end first into the countershaft from the hub side.

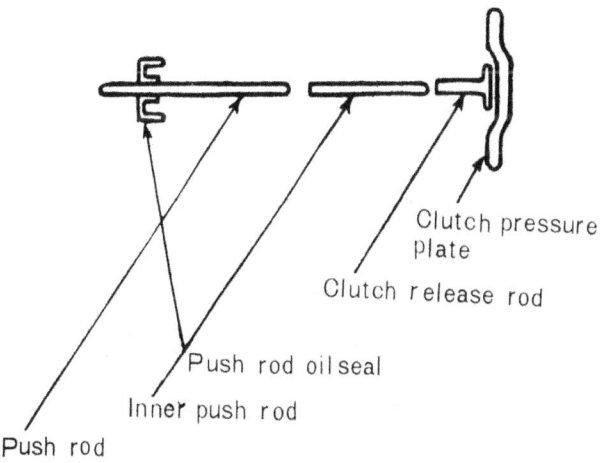

**Fig. 52**
INSTALLING CLUTCH PUSH RODS

## P. Installing Electrical Epuipment

Pull up the carbon brushes before installing the stator assembly and then return them to their proper place after the stator assembly is fitted.

Adjust ignition timing and the contact breaker points gap properly after fitting the starter dynamo. (See "Adjusting Ignition Timing" section)

## Q. Installing Cylinders

Lubricate the pistons generously with oil before fitting the cylinders over the pistons. Be sure to fit the piston rings in the proper position on the pistons, and do not confuse the top and second rings. See Fig. 53. When tightening cylinders and cylinder head bolts and nuts, be sure to tighten them diagonally, not in sequence.

Use the kick starter lever to check the piston movement.

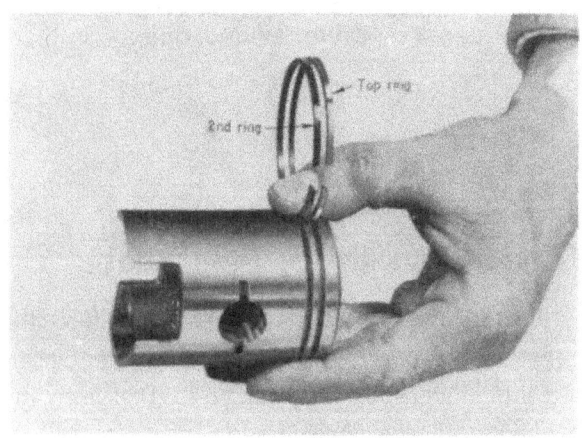

Fig. 53
TOP & 2ND RINGS

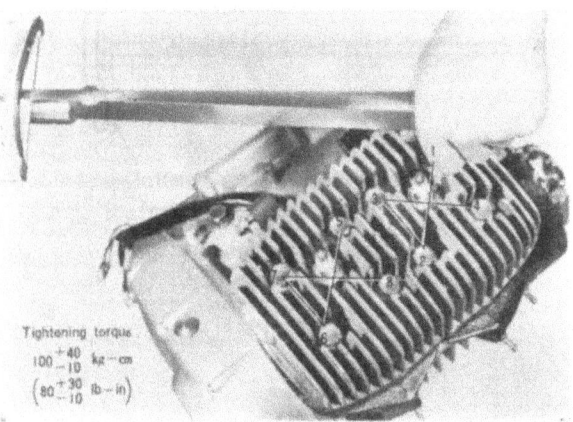

Fig. 54
TIGHTENING CYLINDER HEAD BOLTS

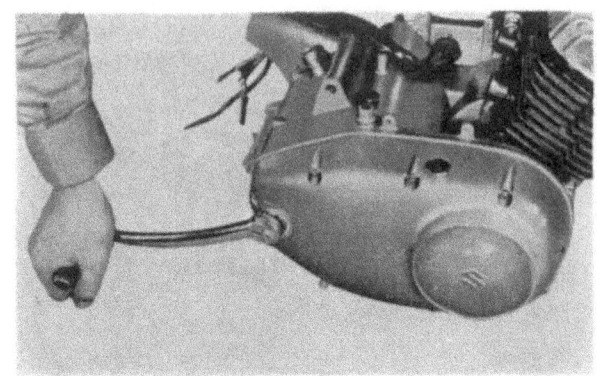

Fig. 55
INSPECTING PISTON MOVEMENT

# 4. Engine Construction and Inspections

## A. Combustion System

### (1) Cylinder Heads

The cylinder heads are made of aluminum alloy and have eleven cooling fins on the outside. They are installed on the cylinders with 8 bolts. The combustion chambers have a squash dome shape and are 14.5 cc in size. They provide good compression, clean fuel burning and give high horsepower.

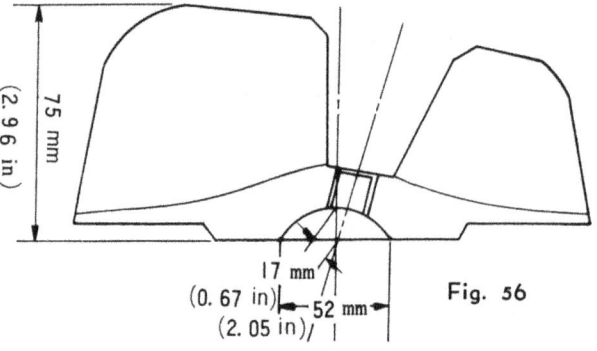

Fig. 56
CYLINDER HEAD

### (2) Head Gaskets

The cylinder head gaskets are made of copper and asbestos and installed between the cylinder heads and cylinders to prevent gas leakage.

The thickness is 3.2 mm (0.13 in) and when the cylinder head is properly tightened the gasket thickness is 2.6 mm (0.10 in).

If worn or damaged gaskets leak compression, the performance of the engine and power are badly affected. Damaged or worn head gaskets must be replaced with new ones.

It is good practice to throw away the old head gaskets and install new ones each time the cylinder head is removed from the cylinder.

## (3) Cylinders

An intake port, exhaust port and two scavenging ports are in the wall of the cylinder. The intake port has a rib in the center to prevent the skirt of the piston from catching on it.

Each cylinder is fitted to the crankcase with 4 studs and nuts. A cylinder base gasket made of special material is placed between the cylinder and crankcase to prevent compression leakage.

The engine port timing is shown in the illustration. The intake port opens at 78° 30' before top dead center and closes at 78° 30' after tdc. The exhaust port opens at 97° 10' after tdc and closes at 97° 10' before tdc.

The carburetor fitting is inclined 15° forward for good intake efficiency.

Worn pistons, piston rings and cylinders cause insufficient compression, decrease of power, increased fuel consumption, bad acceleration and hard starting. Inspect the cylinder bore and parts to determine if they can be used.

Measurement: The bore of a worn cylinder should be measured at four points, in the upper part and lower part of the cylinder and twice near the ports, from front to rear and from side to side.

Action: If the measurements differ more than 0.2 mm (0.00788 in), rebore the cylinder. If the difference is less than 0.2 mm but the cylinder wall is scored or ridged at the top, refinish with a ridge reamer or scraper.

| Measurement | Standard | Limit | Operation |
|---|---|---|---|
| Bore | 52.00–52.019 mm (2.05–2.0495 in) | 52.2 mm (2.0567 in) | rebore |
| Thickness | 6 mm (0.236 in) | 5 mm (0.197 in) | replace |
| Out of Roundness | 0.008 mm (0.0003152 in) | 0.04 mm (0.001576 in) | rebore |
| Difference Between Upper and Lower Parts of Bore | 0.008 mm (0.000315 in) | 0.04 mm (0.001576 in) | rebore |

When reboring the cylinders, the difference in bore measurements between the two cylinders should be less than 0.06 mm (0.002364 in).

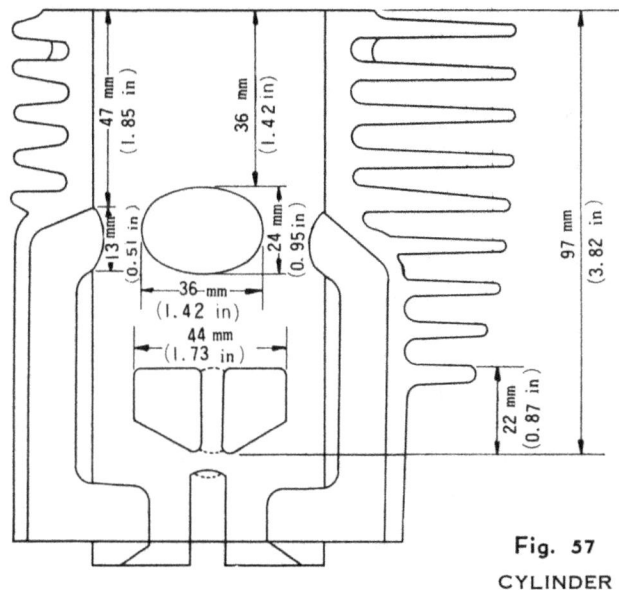

**Fig. 57**
CYLINDER

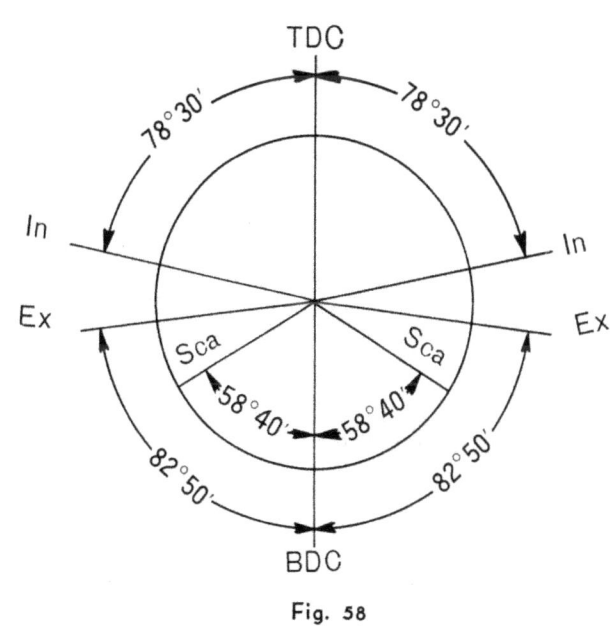

**Fig. 58**
ENGINE PORT TIMING

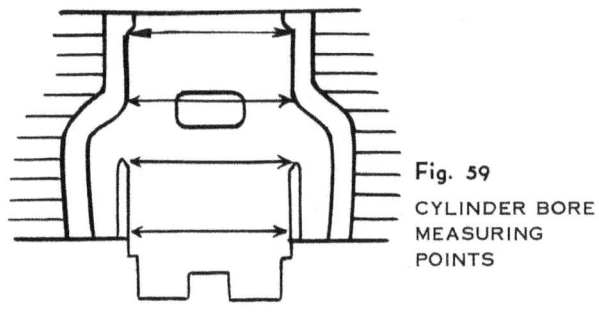

Fig. 59
CYLINDER BORE MEASURING POINTS

### (4) Pistons

The piston receives combustion pressure on its top and converts it to mechanical power. The piston is always exposed to extremely high temperatures. The piston of the T10 motorcycle is made of alsil, which has a low expansion coefficient and high resistance to wear. As the expansion of the piston is largest at the top, the piston is tapered with a smaller diameter at top and slightly larger diameter at the bottom. The piston pin hole is offset 1.5 mm (0.059 in) forward as shown in the illustration. When fitting the piston to the connecting rod, the arrow stamped on the head of the piston must point to the exhaust port.

After removing carbon deposits from the piston, measure the piston with a micrometer as shown in Fig. 62. A defective piston should be replaced with a new one. Inspect the piston

Fig. 60
MEASURING CYLINDER BORE WITH INSIDE MICROMETER

and cylinder for scoring or other damage. Both pistons should be changed at the same time.

| Measurement | Standard | Limit | Operation | Remarks |
| --- | --- | --- | --- | --- |
| Diameter at Top | 51.740~51.760 mm (2.03855~2.03934 in) | | replace | |
| Maximum Diameter | 51.855~51.875 mm (2.04309~2.04388 in) | | replace | 20 mm from bottom of piston |
| Piston Ring Groove Depth | 2.5 mm (0.0985 in) | | | |
| Piston Ring Groove Width | 2.010~2.025 mm (0.07919~0.7978 in) | 2.106 mm (0.08298 in) | replace | |
| Minimum Piston Cylinder Clearance | 0.125 mm (0.00493 in) | 0.3 mm (0.01182 in) | replace | between cylinder bore and piston skirt |
| Piston Pin Hole | 15.984~15.994 mm (0.62977~0.63016 in) | | replace | |

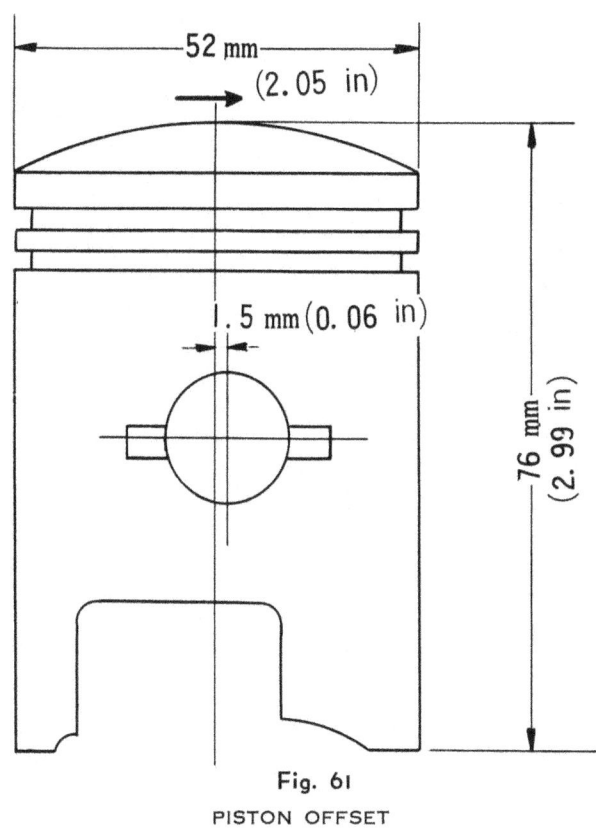

Fig. 61
PISTON OFFSET

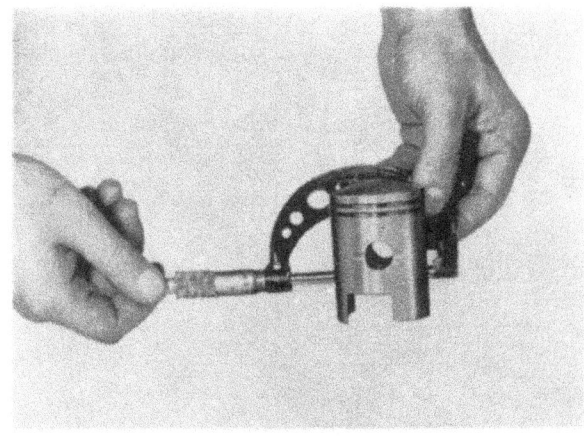

Fig. 62
MEASURING PISTON WITH MICROMETER

### (5) Piston Rings

The T10 engine has two piston rings on each piston. The ring in the upper groove is called the top ring and the one in the lower groove is called the second ring.

The top ring prevnts the combustion pressure in the combustion chamber from leaking into the crankcase. The second ring prevents crankcase pressure from leaking into the combustion chamber and transfers heat from the piston to the cylinder wall.

When the piston ring ends are closed the rings are round, but when the ring ends are open the rings are out of roundness. The piston ring hugs tightly against the cylinder wall because of the expanding force of the ring.

As the top ring is subjected to extremely high temperatuers at all times and is apt to be corroded with combustion gas, hastening its wear, it is chromium plated for higher resistance to wear. As more expanding force per unit is exerted and the surface in contact with the cylinder wall is reduced in the second ring, it is parkerized. A parkerized ring fits the cylinder easily.

The end gap of piston rings must not hit the scavenging ports and exhaust port located in the cylinder wall of a two-cycle engine. The T10 engine has phosphor-bronze piston ring locating pins installed in the piston ring grooves.

Align the piston ring end gap with the locating pin when fitting the piston ring. Fit the correct ring. Do not confuse the top and second rings.

### (6) Inspecting Piston Ring Wear and Tension

Wear or insufficient tension of the piston ring allows it to leak compression, causing piston slap in addition to decreasing power, increasing fuel consumption, causing poor acceleration, hard starting, etc. Check the ring and replace if needed. Replace rings in both cylinders at the same time.

Measurement: The standard end gap of both the top and second ring is 0.15 ~ 0.35 mm (0.0059 ~ 0.0138 in) when the ring is installed squarely in the cylinder bore.

To check the piston ring end gap, insert the ring into the lower part of the cylinder at the position of the piston bottom dead center

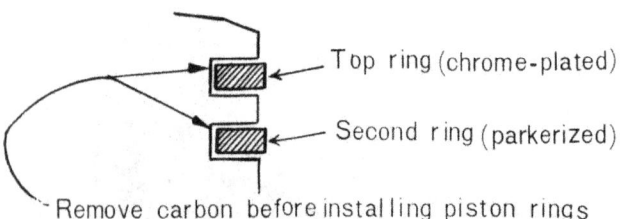

**Fig. 63**
PISTON RINGS IN GROOVES

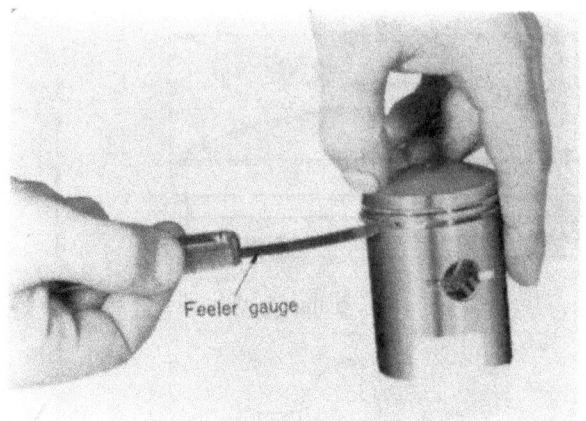

**Fig. 65**
MEASURING PISTON RING SIDE CLEARANCE

**Fig. 64**
MEASURING PISTON RING END GAP

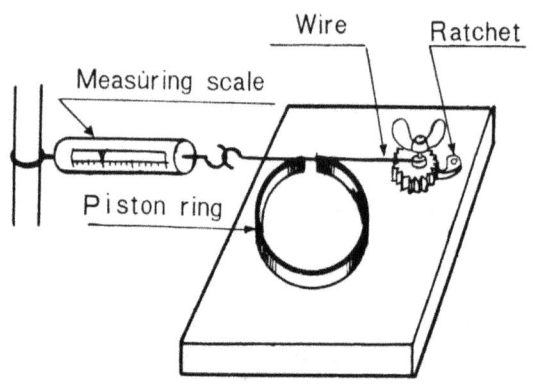

**Fig. 66**
MEASURING PISTON RING TENSION

and measure the end gap with a feeler gauge.

When the clearance between ring and piston ring groove increases it allows leakage of compression. Fit the piston ring into the piston groove as shown in Fig. 65 and measure the side clearance with a feeler gauge.

When the piston ring tension decreases, it does not fit against the cylinder wall tightly and allows compression to leak. Check piston ring tension as shown in Fig. 66. Turn the knob of the ratchet slowly and read the scale when the end gap is the standard 0.15 mm (0.0059 in).

| Measurement | Standard | Limit | Operation |
| --- | --- | --- | --- |
| Thickness | 1.970~1.990 mm (0.0762~0.0784 in) | 1.790 mm (0.07053 in) | replace |
| Width | 2.0~2.2 mm (0.0788~0.0867 in) | | |
| Tension | 0.6~0.8 kg (1.32~1.76 lbs) | 0.4 kg (0.88 lbs) | replace |
| End Gap | 0.15~0.35 mm (0.0059~0.0138 in) | 1.0 mm (0.0394 in) | replace |
| Side Clearance | 0.020~0.055 mm (0.00079~0.0021 in) | 0.15 mm (0.00591 in) | replace |

## (7) Piston Pins

The piston pin connects the piston to the connecting rod and transmits the pressure from the piston to the rod smoothly. The piston pin in the T10 engine is made of chromium-molybdenum steel and is carburizing quenched, so that it is extremely hard and can endure strong pressure and friction.

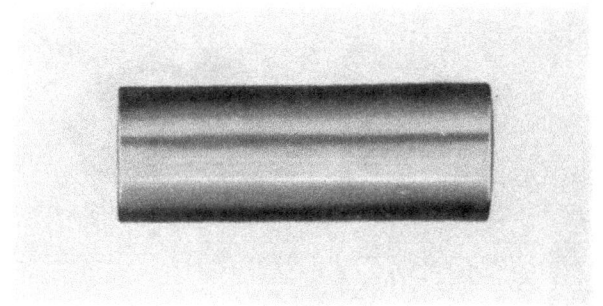

**Fig. 67**
PISTON PIN

Piston Pin Size

| | |
|---|---|
| Outside Diameter | 15.989~15.995 mm (0.62997~0.6302 in) |
| Length | 42.9~43.1 mm (1.690~1.698 in) |
| Clearance between Piston Pin Hole and Piston Pin | −0.005~+0.011 mm (−0.00020~+0.00043 in) |
| Out of Roundness | below 0.002 mm (0.000079 in) |

## (8) Crankcase

The crankcase is made of aluminum alloy which is of high quality, light, compact and can be mass produced. An outstanding feature of the T10 engine is that the crankcase can be separated into upper and lower parts so that installing the crankshaft and transmission gears is easy. Liquid gasket is applied on the crankcase joining surfaces and the two parts of the crankcase are held by 15 bolts so that there is no warpage or leakage problem. The tightening order of the crankcase bolts is stamped on the bottom of the crankcase. Tighten the bolts in the correct sequence with the specified torque.

Tightening Torque

6 mm bolts
   ... 100 kg-cm ( 85 lb-in)

8 mm bolts
   ... 200 kg-cm (170 lb-in)

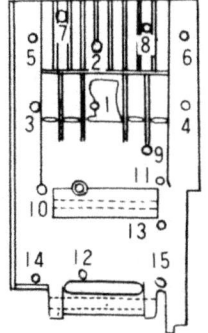

**Fig. 68**
TIGHTENING ORDER OF CRANKCASE BOLTS

## B. Power Transmission System

### (1) Clutch

The clutch is an important part of the engine, situated between the crankshaft and transmission gears. The clutch transmits or breaks transmission of engine power to the gears. The clutch assembly must have a long life and not slip or drag.

The clutch consists of cork plates, steel plates, clutch housing and a clutch sleeve hub which is light in weight. The clutch is installed on the right end of the countershaft.

When the clutch lever mounted on the handlebar is squeezed the clutch wire is pulled, turning the release screw (1) in the release screw guide so that the clutch push rods (2) installed in the countershaft are pushed against the release rod (3) which moves the pressure plate (4) out so that the clutch disengages.

Engine power is transmitted in the order of primary pinion, primary gear (5), cork plates (6), steel plates (7), countershaft, drive shaft, engine sprocket, drive chain, rear sprocket and rear wheel.

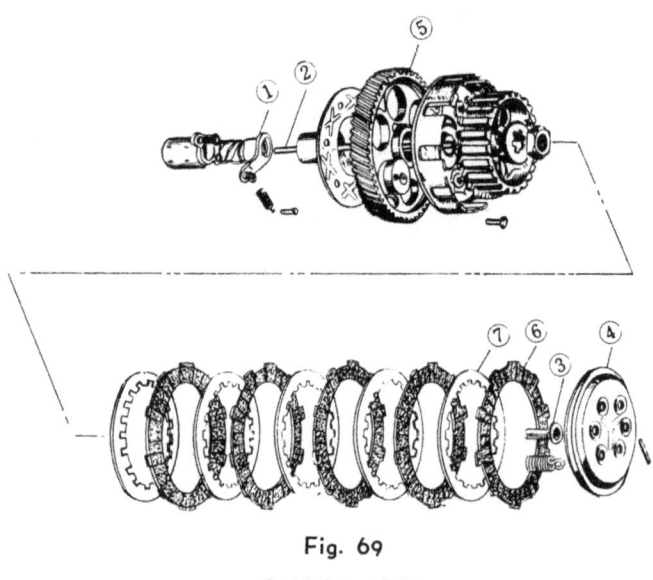

Fig. 69
CLUTCH ASSY

countershaft bearings.

The clutch housing spacer has four oil holes as shown in Fig. 70. This spacer provides good lubrication to the primary gear and prevents it from seizing.

The release screw is made of steel with high resistance to heat.

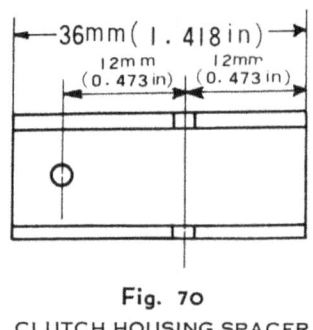

Fig. 70
CLUTCH HOUSING SPACER

The T10 clutch has five cork plates and five steel plates to increase transmitting torque. The outside diameter of the clutch sleeve hub is 142 mm (5.59in). The clutch has an aluminum hub instead of steel. Reducing the weight of the hub increases acceleration performance, reduces gear noise and prolongs the life of the

(2) Inspecting Clutch Springs

If the length of the clutch springs differs the clutch is difficult to adjust and defective operation results. Check the clutch springs for length, tension, etc.

| | |
|---|---|
| Effective Number of Coils | 11.5 |
| Outside Diameter | 12 mm (0.473 in) |
| Spring Strength | 1.0 kg/mm (7.2 lb/in) |
| Installed Load | 10.7 kg (22.0 lb) |
| Installed Length | 43 mm (1.69 in) |

Fig. 71
CLUTCH SPRING LENGTF

(3) Inspecting Clutch Plates

Check the clearance and inspect for ridged wearing between the teeth of the clutch cork plates and clutch housing grooves and between the teeth of the clutch steel plates and clutch sleeve hub grooves.

Excessive clearance or ridged wearing prevents smooth clutch operation as well as producing noise in the clutch. Uneven contact or warpage of cork plates or steel plates or dirt on the plates causes the clutch to slip or

drag. Inspect the steel plates on a flat surface for warpage as shown in Fig. 72. Repair with a press. Cork plates can be repaired by grinding the cork surface with emery paper attached to a flat surface. Replace the cork plates if oil has penetrated into the cork. Worn clutch plate surfaces cause the clutch to slip, so measure the thickness of the plates with calipers to compare with the standard. If the thicknes is below 3.2 mm (0.126 in), replace with new plates.

Fig. 72
INSPECTING CLUTCH STEEL PLATE
FLATNESS ON A FLAT SURFACE

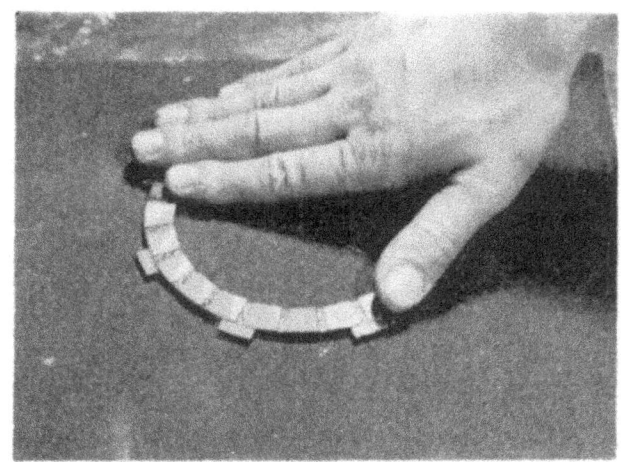

Fig 73
GRINDING CLUTCH CORK PLATE

## Clutch Cork Plates

| Measurement | Standard | Limit |
|---|---|---|
| Thickness | 3.5 ± 0.1 mm (0.138 ± 0.0039 in) | below 3.2 mm (0.126 in) |
| Warpage | below 0.25 mm (0.000985 in) | out of std. |

## Clutch Steel Plates

| Measurement | Standard | Limit |
|---|---|---|
| Thickness | 1.6~1.8 mm (0.06304~0.07092 in) | |
| Warpage | below 0.1 mm (0.00394 in) | out of std. |

### (4) Inspecting Clutch Sleeve Hub

The clutch sleeve hub is spline-connected to the transmission countershaft. Excessive play in the spline connection badly affects clutch operation. Replace the countershaft or clutch sleeve hub if play in the spline connection is excessive.

Turning Direction Play

Limit . . . . . . . . . . 0.5 mm (0.0197 in)

Allowance . . . . . . . . 0.2 mm (0.0079 in)

### (5) Inspecting Clutch Housing

If the groove of the clutch housing is ridged in wearing, it catches the clutch plate teeth and causes the clutch to drag.

### (6) Transmission

Motorcycles are not operated under the same conditions at all times, so a transmission combining the proper torque and rpm to handle different riding conditions is required. There are many types of transmissions, but a constant-mesh system is used for most multi-speed machines. The T10 has a constant-mesh four speed transmission. Operation of this type of transmission is very simple. Depressing the front part of the change lever shifts into a higher gear and depressing the rear part shifts into a lower gear.

Engine power is transmitted in the order of primary pinion (installed on the right end of the crankshaft), primary gear (installed on the right end of the countershaft), countershaft, drive shaft, engine sprocket, drive chain, rear sprocket and rear wheel.

| | | |
|---|---|---|
| 1. | Low Gear | Turns freely on drive shaft |
| 2. | Third Gear | Spline-fitted on drive shaft, moved by shifting fork |
| 3. | Second Gear | Turns freely on drive shaft, fixed with a circlip |
| 4. | Top Gear | Unit constructed with drive shaft |
| 5. | Low Pinion | Unit constructed with countershaft |
| 6. | Third Pinion | Turns freely on countershaft, fixed with a circlip |
| 7. | Second Pinion | Spline-fitted on countershaft, moved by shifting fork |
| 8. | Top Pinion | Turns freely on countershaft |

| Speed | Gear Moved | Power Transmission | Reduction Ratio (Overall) |
|---|---|---|---|
| Low | (2) to (1) | (5) – (1) – (9) | 2.36 (20.8) |
| Second | (2) to (3) | (7) – (3) – (9) | 1.45 (12.15) |
| Third | (7) to (6) | (6) – (2) – (9) | 0.96 ( 7.85) |
| Top | (7) to (8) | (8) – (4) – (9) | 0.74 ( 6.06) |

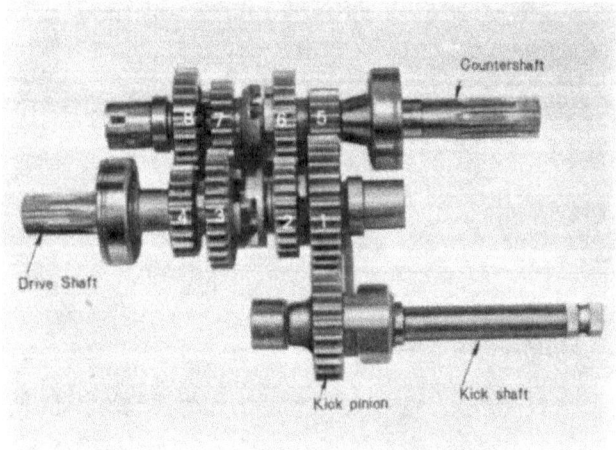

**Fig. 74**
TRANSMISSION GEARS

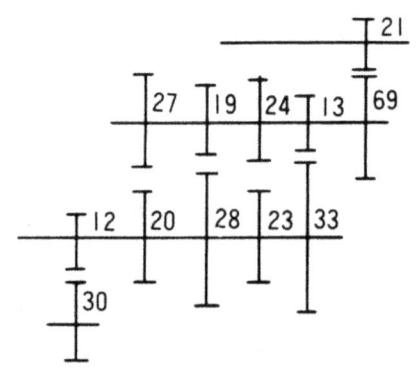

**Fig. 75**
NUMBERS OF GEAR TEETH

A 12-tooth engine sprocket and 30-tooth rear sprocket are standard on the T10. These sprockets are available as optional parts:

| Part No. | Part Name | Remarks |
| --- | --- | --- |
| T10-2511S11 | Engine Sprocket | 11-tooth, for heavy loads |
| T10-6441S28 | Rear Sprocket | 28-tooth, for high speeds |

Excessive play in worn splined parts of the shafts causes noise and defective gear engaging and hastens the wear of the transmission gears. To inspect the clearance, insert an accurately sized piano wire into the clearance between the splined shaft and gear.

Splined Part Turning Direction Play

| Limit | 0.5 mm (0.0197 in) |
| --- | --- |
| Allowance | 0.2 mm (0.0079 in) |

If the play exceeds the limit, replace the shaft or gear. Excessive wear, damaged or improper engaging surfaces of gears causes noise during operation and increases resistance, which hastens the wear and damage of gears. When excessive play is found in a gear, replace it with a new one. When improper engaging surface is found, replace it.

In addition to the natural wear of gears, worn shafts and shifting forks, play in fitting parts, improper gear engaging, insufficient lubrication, etc., causes wear of gears.

### (7) Kick Starter

A kick starter is provided for emergency use if the electric starter does not work.

When the kick starter lever is depressed the kick starter shaft (A) turns in a counterclockwise direction when seen from the kick starter lever end of the shaft. When the kick starter shaft (A) turns counterclockwise, the kick starter pawl installed on the (B) part of the kick starter shaft engages the teeth on the inside of the kick starter pinion and the kick starter pinion (C) turns, as the kick starter pawl is inserted into the side of the kick starter shaft and moves at a right angle to it.

The kick starter pinion moves low gear (D) with which it is engaged and the crankshaft (E) is turned in the order of low pinion (F), primary gear (G), primary pinion and crankshaft.

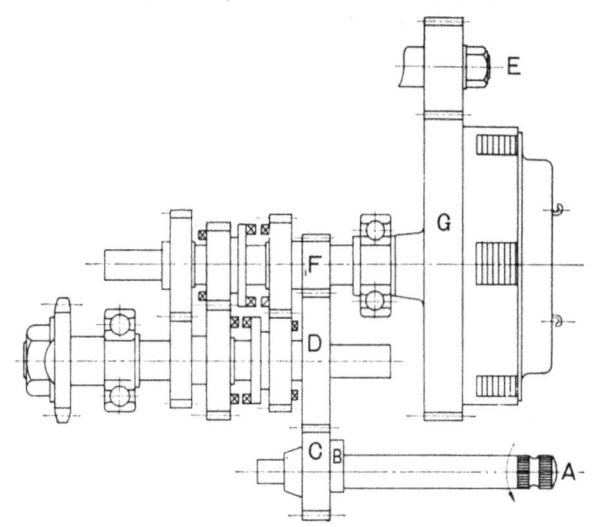

**Fig. 76**
KICK STARTER OPERATION

## C. Fuel System

### (1) Carburetors

Two Villiers VM 20 carburetors are installed on the T10. In twin-cylinder engines with a single carburetor, sometimes one cylinder fails to operate because of an uneven distribution of fuel, but a twin carburetor system supplies fuel to both cylinders effectively and this problem is resolved, performance is increased and fuel consumption is decreased.

The compact VM 20 carburetor has a float chamber unit constructed with the mixing chamber. The float chamber is located under the mixing chamber and the air shutter is installed in the carburetor air intake venturi. A double-float decreases the effect of vibrations, limits the change of fuel level in the chamber when the motorcycle is leaned to the side and helps keep fuel from overflowing.

(A) Operation

The carburetor meters the amount of fuel which the engine requires.

The carburetor supplies a proper fuel/air mixture to the engine according to varying operating conditions.

To maintain steady performance, carburetor parts must be resistant to wear.

The carburetors mounted on the T10 conform to these requirements and develop high performance from the engine.

(B) Specifications

| | |
|---|---|
| Main jet | ♯70 |
| Air jet | 1.3 mm (0.051 in)⌀ |
| Jet needle | 24A, fourth groove |
| Needle jet | N-6 |
| Throttle valve cutaway | 2.5 mm (0.099 in)⌀ |
| Pilot jet | ♯30 *♯25 |
| Pilot outlet | 0.6 mm (0.024 in)⌀ |
| Pilot air adjusting screw | 1½ *1¾ |
| By-pass | 1.4 mm (0.055 in)⌀ |
| Valve seat | 2.5 mm (0.099 in)⌀ |

Specifications marked with asterisks (*) are for motorcycles with engine numbers higher than 11825.

(C) Construction

a  Main Channel

Air coming through the air cleaner is inhaled into the engine through the carburetor intake (1) and flows past the throttle valve (2). Vacuum is induced by the air flow around the jet needle (3) and fuel is sucked up through the main jet (4) from the float chamber. Air entering through the air jet (5) meets the air flow around the needle jet (6). As the air flows at a high speed, the fuel is atomized into a fine mist. This meets the main air flow and mixes with it. The fuel/air mixture is inhaled into the engine.

b  Slow Channel

When the engine is idling, the throttle valve is lowered almost to the bottom (0~1/8 throttle opening). Air is inhaled mainly through the pilot air inlet (7) for idling adjustment. Air entering through the pilot air inlet is metered by the pilot air adjusting screw and sucks up fuel through the pilot jet installed for idling adjustment. A richer fuel mixture than that supplied by the main channel is inhaled into the engine through the pilot outlet (9). The fuel and air mixture ratio in the slow channel is controlled by the pilot air adjusting screw.

(D) Cleaning Carburetors

a  Removing

- Close fuel cock.
- Remove choke lever with screw driver.
- Remove carburetor covers with screw driver.
- Remove air cleaner tube clamps with screw driver and disconnect air cleaner tubes.
- Remove carburetor union bolts with 12 mm wrench, and gaskets.
- Loosen outlet clamps with screw driver.
- Pull carburetors off of cylinder inlet stubs.
- Remove mixing chamber cap holders and pull from carburetors along with throttle vales, jet needles and jet needle clips.
- Remove carburetors from engine.

b  Disassembling

- Remove float chamber body with phillips screw driver, and take out float chamber gasket if it is damaged.
- Remove float pin stopper and float.
- Remove needle valve circlip with screw driver and take out needle and spring.

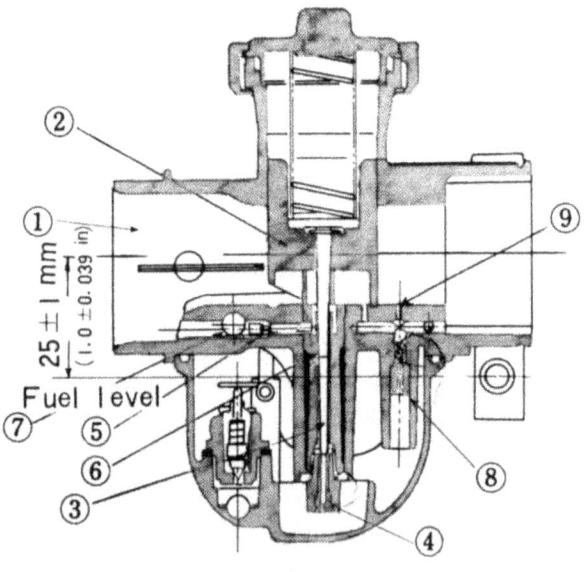

Fig. 77
CARBURETOR OPERATION

- Remove needle valve seat with 9 mm wrench, and gasket.
- Remove main jet with 6 mm wrench and needle jet stop washer.
- Push needle jet out of top of body.
- Remove throttle valve stop screw and spring with fingers or phillips screw driver.
- Remove pilot air adjusting screw and spring with phillips screw driver.

c   Inspecting and Servicing

- Check needle valve tapered end for wear. Replace if worn or stepped. Replace worn gasket.
- Shake float to see if there is fuel inside. If there is, float leaks and must be replaced.
- Check union bolt gaskets for wear and replace if needed.
- Wash all parts with cleaning solvent and dry.
- Blow compressed air through all jets and the hole in the union bolt to make sure they are not clogged.
- Check float chamber gasket for wear and replace if needed.
- Check mixing chamber cap gasket for wear and replace if needed.
- Check throttle cable adjuster cap for cracks, etc., and replace if needed.
- Insert throttle valve in mixing chamber and check for play to see if throttle valve is worn. Replace worn, scored or scratched throttle valve.
- Check jet needle for scoring or scratches and replace if damaged.

d   Assembling

- Insert needle jet from top of mixing chamber and push into position with finger.
- Insert main jet and fit needle jet stop washer.
- Fit pilot air adjusting screw and spring.
- Fit throttle valve stop screw and spring.
- Place gasket in position and fit needle valve seat. Insert spring, fit valve and insert circlip.
- Install float and float pin stopper.
- Place float chamber gasket into position in slot on chamber rim.
- Fit float chamber to mixing chamber with two screws and washers.
- Attach throttle valve and needle jet, throttle valve spring, mixing chamber cap and mixing chamber top to throttle cable.

e   Installing

- Insert throttle valve into mixing chamber, and tighten mixing chamber cap holder.

CAUTION : The throttle valve must be fitted with the groove on the opposite side from the cutaway fitting over the pin inside the mixing chamber.

- Fit carburetors on engine inlet stubs and tighten outlet clamps with screw driver.
- Fit carburetor union bolts with 12 mm wrench. Be sure both gaskets are fitted. Replace worn gaskets.
- Fit air cleaner tubes and tighten clamps with screw driver.
- Fit choke lever with screw driver.
- Open fuel cock and check to see that fuel flows to the carburetors.

( E )   Tips on Mounting Carburetors

The two carburetors should be installed in an absolutely horizontal position. Connect the choke levers inside the carburetors as shown in the illustration. The two carburetors are not interchangable, as the location of ticklers, throttle valve stop screws, pilot air adjusting screws and fuel line joints are different. The carburetor with the tickler on the right side when viewed from the air intake is mounted on the right cylinder and the carburetor with the tickler on the left is mounted on the left cylinder.

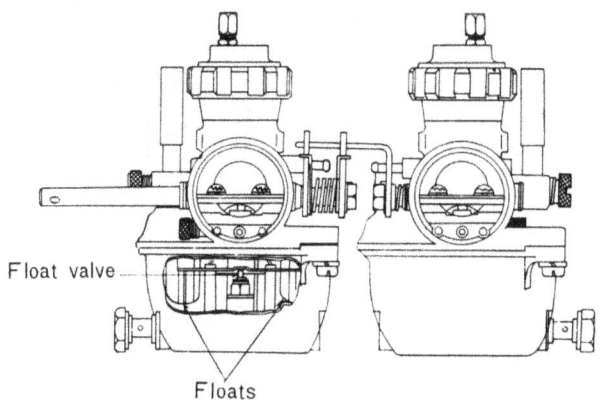

**Fig. 78**
CARBURETORS

( F ) Adjusting Idling

a  Preparations

Clip the jet needle in the standard groove (4th from top) of the needle.

Adjust play in both right and left throttle cables to 0.5~1 mm (0.02~0.04 in) with the throttle cable adjusters on the carburetors. If the throttle cables are not adjusted equally, the engine rpm will differ when the throttle grip is moved slightly from the idling position. Further, if the play in the two cables differs considerably, the engine rpm at medium and high speeds will differ.

Warm the engine up for 2~3 minutes.

b  Adjusting

Remove the spark plug cap on one cylinder. Turn the pilot air adjusting screw on the other side down to the bottom, then turn it back out $1\frac{3}{4}$ turns.

Start the engine, which, of course, will fire on only one cylinder since the spark plug cap is off of the cylinder other than one being adjusted.

Adjust the throttle valve stop screw until the engine runs at its lowest rpm.

Turn the pilot air adjusting screw in and out within the range of $\frac{1}{2}$ of a turn from the standard ($1\frac{3}{4}$ turns out from the bottom). The engine rpm will increase and decrease in accordance with the turning of the screw. Find the position where the engine runs regular ly and smoothly at the lowest rpm, and fix the screw there.

After adjusting the pilot air adjusting screw, adjust the throttle valve stop screw again and determine the engine idling rpm while running on one cylinder.

When one cylinder has been adjusted, adjust the other cylinder in the same manner.

After adjusting the two cylinders separately, operate both cylinders at the same time. Idling rpm will be rather high. Turn both throttle valve stop screws out the same amount and adjust the idling rpm.

c  Balancing Right and Left Cylinders

The right and left carburetors can be adjusted by adjusting the throttle cables, pilot air adjusting screws and throttle valve stop screws, but if the density or amount of exhaust fumes from the two cylinders is not the same adjust the engine in the following manner: Gradually turn the pilot air adjusting screw out on the cylinder which exhausts richer fumes and turn the pilot air adjusting screw in gradually on the cylinder which exhausts leaner fumes. The amount to turn each screw depends on the condition of the engine, but do not turn the screw in beyond the position where it is turned out $1\frac{1}{4}$ turns from the bottom and do not turn it out where it is more than $2\frac{1}{4}$ turns from the bottom.

Keep the difference between the position of the two screws to within one full turn. An excessive difference causes over-heating or increases fuel consumption.

(G)  Adjusting Fuel/Air Mixture

a  Too Rich Fuel

The exhaust fume is bluish white and dense. Fuel blows back into the carburetor. The motorcycle feels sluggish when running. The spark plug becomes black. (When too cold a plug is used or the motorcycle is ridden at extremely low speeds, the same spark plug condition is produced. Replace the spark plug with one of the proper heat range.)

b  Too Lean Fuel

Idling is not smooth. The engine is apt to overheat. Engine rpm fluctuates even if the throttle grip is held steady. Acceleration is bad. The spark plug becomes white. (When too hot a plug is used or the motorcycle is ridden at extremely high speeds, the same spark plug condition is produced. Replace the spark plug with one of the proper heat range.)

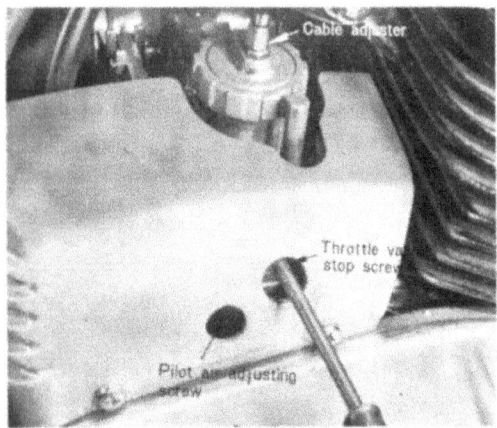

**Fig. 79**
ADJUSTING CARBURETION

(H) Adjusting Carburetor for All Speeds

a   Adjusting for High Speeds

From $\frac{3}{4}$ to full throttle opening, the mixture ratio can be adjusted by the main jet. When the throttle grip is turned back slightly from the full throttle position, if the engine rpm increases the fuel mixture is too lean and if it decreases the mixture is proper or too rich. When the mixture is too lean, use a higher numbered main jet than the standard #70.

b   Adjusting for Medium Speeds

From $\frac{1}{4}$ to $\frac{3}{4}$ throttle opening, the mixture ratio can be adjusted by changing the position of the jet needle or by the throttle valve cutaway.

• Adjusting with Jet Needle

If the exhaust fumes are bluish white caused by a too rich fuel mixture, lower the jet needle one notch by fitting the clip in the next higher groove on the jet needle. If the engine seems to be dragging when the motorcycle is accelerating or running, it indicates that the fuel mixture is too lean. Raise the jet needle by one notch.

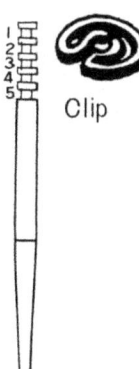

**Fig. 80**
JET NEEDLE & CLIP

• Adjusting with Throttle Valve Cutaway

A higher numbered throttle valve cutaway gives a leaner mixture and a lower numbered one a richer mixture. The standard throttle valve cutaway for the T10 is 2.5 mm (0.099 in). A different size throttle valve cutaway, however, seriously affects engine operation at below $\frac{1}{4}$ throttle opening. Do not change the throttle valve cutaway unless it is urgently necessary.

c   Adjusting for Low Speeds

From $\frac{1}{8}$ to $\frac{1}{4}$ throttle opening, the mixture ratio can be adjusted with the pilot air adjusting screw and the throttle valve stop screw. Refer to the Adjusting Idling section above.

(I)   Carburetor Adjusting Chart

| Throttle Opening | Too Rich Fuel | Too Lean Fuel |
|---|---|---|
| $0 \sim \frac{1}{8}$ | turn pilot air adjusting screw out | turn pilot air adjusting screw in |
| * $\frac{1}{8} \sim \frac{1}{4}$ | use throttle valve with bigger cutaway | use throttle valve with smaller cutaway |
| $\frac{1}{4} \sim \frac{3}{4}$ | lower jet needle | raise jet needle |
| $\frac{3}{4} \sim$ full | use smaller numbered main jet | use larger numbered main jet |

CAUTION: Do not change the throttle valve cutaway unless there is an urgent necessity. Adjust the carburetor by using the other methods.

(2) **Throttle Cable Connector**

The two throttle cables connected to the two carburetors are connected inside the throttle cable connector under the front part of the fuel tank to a single throttle cable going to the throttle grip on the handlebar.

(A)   Construction

The sliding piece moves in the connector tube as shown in the illustration and opens and closes the throttle valves on the carburetors. Two carburetor side throttle cables are fitted to the connector sliding piece on one end and on the other the handlebar side throttle cable which goes to the throttle grip is fitted.

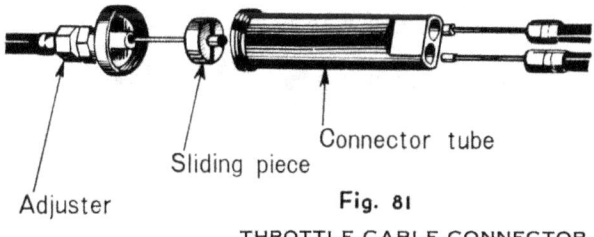

**Fig. 81**
THROTTLE CABLE CONNECTOR

(3) **Adjusting Throttle Cables**

The carburetor side throttle cables can be adjusted by the cable adjusters on the top of the carburetors.

The handlebar side throttle cable can be adjusted by the adjuster on the throttle cable connector.

Be sure to lubricate the throttle cable connector sliding piece with grease and check to see that the piece moves smoothly when fitting the throttle cables.

# FRAME

The frame of the T10 is made of pressed steel and is of the stressed skin type construction. The frame is a product of long years of research. It is light and strong and at the same time is easy to produce and handle. A head pipe with ball races pressed into both ends is welded to the frame. The ball races and steel balls give safe and easy steering. Electrical equipment is installed on the middle of the frame where vibration is the least to ensure high performance. Electrical equipment is easily accessible by removing the frame right cover. A tool kit is fitted inside the frame left cover so that it is easily accessible.

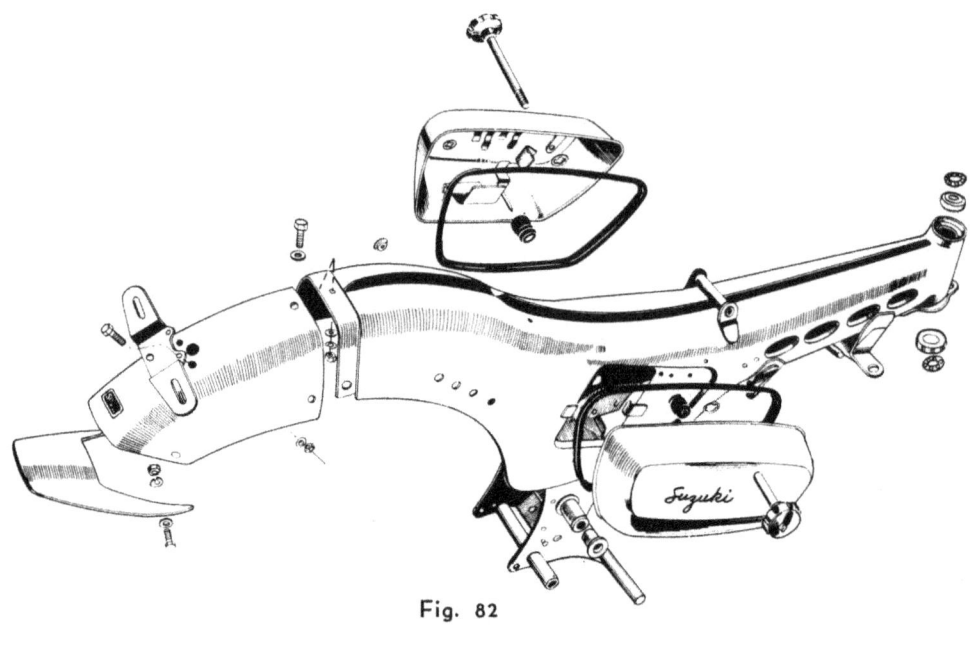

Fig. 82

FRAME

## 1. Inspecting and Servicing Frame

Check all welded points. Check for cracks, damage or deforming from the head pipe to the rear fender. Particularly, if the motorcycle has been in a collision or serious accident, check the frame carefully. If the frame is cracked, damaged or deformed, repair or replace according to the amount of damage.

### A. Twist and Alignment Inspection

The stability and handling of the motorcycle will be badly affected if the frame is twisted or out of alignment or the head pipe is off center. Check carefully and repair or replace, as needed.

### B. Ball Races and Steel Balls

Check ball races and steel balls in the head pipe of a used frame particularly carefully. Eccentric wear or a cracked ball race badly affects the handling of the motorcycle. Replace all ball races and steel balls when any defect is found.

To remove a ball race, fit a rod against the bottom of the race from inside the head pipe and strike the rod gently with a hammer.

( 1 ) Installing Ball Races

Do not use new steel balls with old ball races or new ball races with old steel balls. If any defect is found on either ball races or steel balls, replace both together.

Wash ball races and steel balls with gasoline or cleaning solvent and dry with a clean cloth. Apply fresh grease. Be sure sand, dirt or other particles are not mixed in the grease, as this will cause rapid and dangerous wear. Be sure the ball races are kept clean at all times. Install ball races by pressing or tapping them into the head pipe, then pack with grease and fit steel balls.

## 2. Tires

Comfortable riding is assured by the use of 3.00″ tires on both front and rear wheels.

The front wheel mounts a ribbed tire to prevent side slip and the rear wheel has a semi-block tire to minimize wheel spin and utilize the power of the engine effectively. When mounting the tires, be sure they are put on the proper wheel.

Excessive tire inflation causes hard riding, and damages the tire. Low tire pressure causes internal damage to the tire and makes it easier to pick up nails to cause punctures or break the tire cords on sharp objects. Excessive overloads on the tire shorten tire life extremely. Tires should always be used with correct pressure and loads.

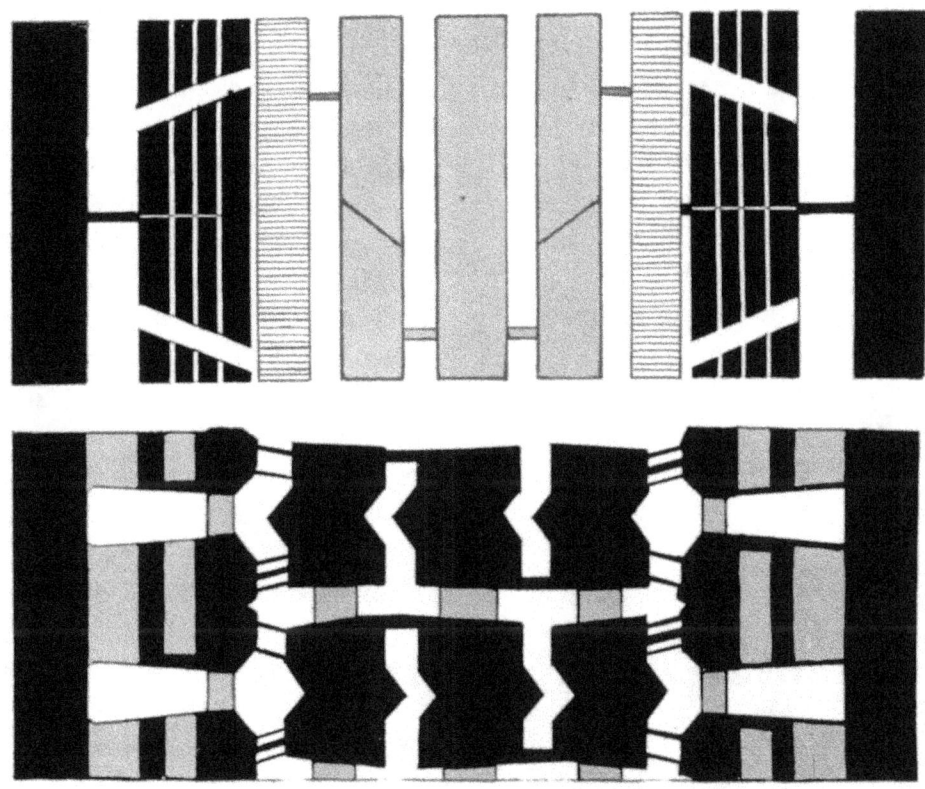

**Fig. 83**
TIRE TREADS

Standard Tire Pressure

|  | Front | Rear |
|---|---|---|
| Solo Riding | 1.1~1.3 kg/cm² (16~18 psi) | 1.8~2.0 kg/cm² (26~28 psi) |
| Dual Riding | 1.1~1.3 kg/cm² (16~18 psi) | 2.3~2.4 kg/cm² (32~34 psi) |

If the tread is worn excessively, the tire slips and skids during riding, punctures occur easily and heat radiation becomes poor, so that riding with a worn tire is dangerous. Replace worn tires with new ones.

The T10 mounts light and strong wheel rims reinforced with welding, as shown in Fig. 84. Each wheel has 36 spokes. The spokes are inserted in the wheel hub drum from the inside and outside alternately so that the wheel rim is stable and does not shake. The spokes are fixed to the rim with nipples. The nipples should be tightened every 3,000 km (1,900 miles), as they can loosen during running. Use a nipple wrench and tighten the spokes evenly.

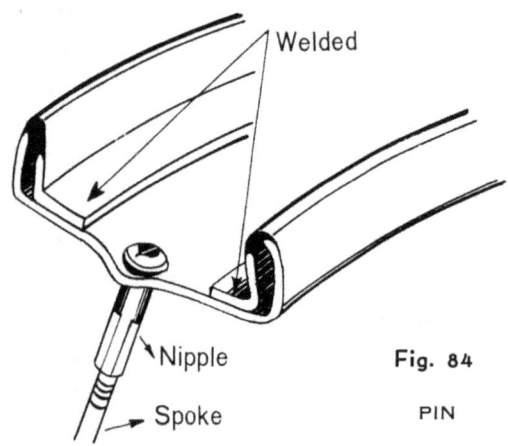

Fig. 84
PIN

## A. Removing and Fitting Tires and Inner Tubes

To remove a tire from the wheel rim, first remove the wheel from the motorcycle. Take off inner tube valve cap and valve stem lock nut. Loosen valve stem core with the tip of valve cap and let the air out of the inner tube. Place the wheel as shown in Fig. 85 and insert tire lever between the tire and wheel rim. Push down on the lever and remove the tire from the wheel. It is best to use two tire levers.

When the bead on one side has been completely removed from the rim, push the inner tube valve stem out of the stem hole on the rim and pull out the inner tube.

Fig. 85
REMOVING TIRE WITH TIRE LEVERS

After repairing the inner tube, align the tube valve stem with the stem hole on the rim and fit the inner tube inside the tire. Be sure that the tube is not twisted. Insert the valve stem through the hole and fit the valve stem lock nut. To fit the tire on the rim, press the tire in on one side and then fit the other side by using a tire lever.

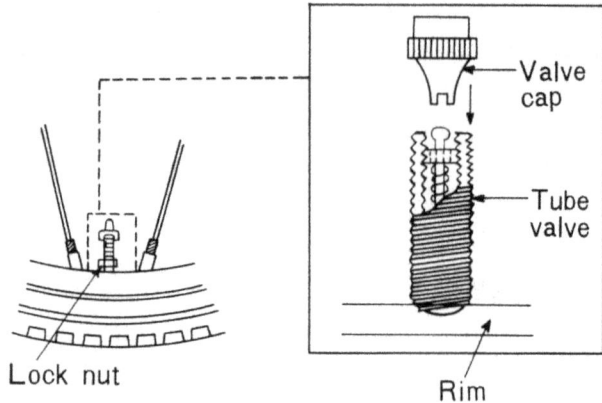

Fig. 86
INNER TUBE VALVE

CAUTION: The tire bead is very hard and it is a tight fit in the rim, but do not treat it roughly.

After fitting the tire, insert the valve core and inflate the tire. When inflating the tire, insert air slowly and strike the tire or bounce it to make the inner tube fit properly. It is best to let out the air once again after the tire is inflated and inflate it again to make sure the inner tube positions properly.

CAUTION: The valve stem must be at right angles to the rim. After the tire is inflated, tighten the inner tube valve stem lock nut firmly and fit the valve cap. Check to see if the valve leaks before fitting the valve cap. If it does, replace the valve core with a new one.

CAUTION: When removing and fitting the inner tube, be careful not to damage the valve stem threads. Take care not to damage tire or inner tube with tire lever.

## 3. Air Cleaners

Two air cleaners, one for each cylinder, are fitted to the frame with bolts. The air cleaners have a sufficient capacity to match the piston displacement of the engine, so air intake efficiency is excellent. The air cleaners are a double paper type which collect dust and dirt completely, supplying only clean air to the engine. Clean the air cleaners every 3,000 km (1,900 miles) and replace every 10,000 km (6,000 miles).

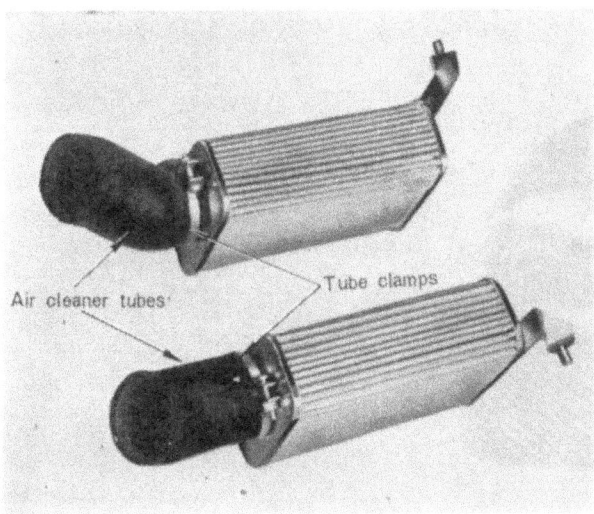

**Fig. 87**
AIR CLEANERS

## 4. Exhaust System

If exhaust fumes are expelled directly into the air an unpleasant noise is produced, so mufflers are installed on the end of the expansion chambers as shown in Fig. 88. Exhaust gases expand slightly in the muffler and exhaust noise is reduced.

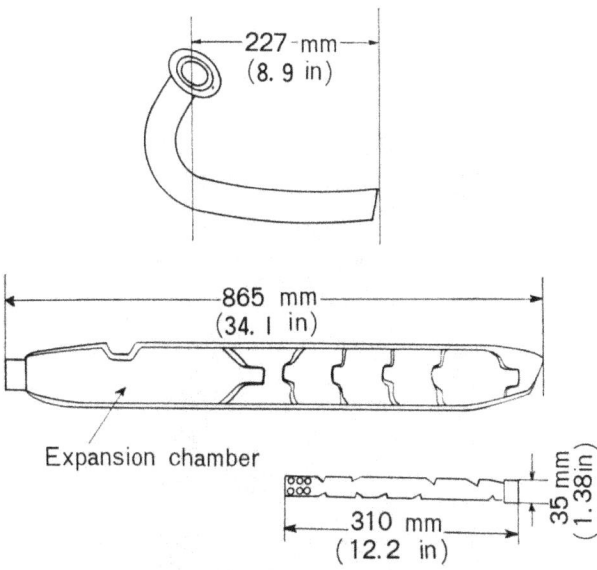

**Fig. 88**
EXHAUST SYSTEM

An expansion chamber in front of the muffler increases the output of the engine by utilizing the pulsation effect.

If carbon accumulates in the muffler baffle pipe, back pressure on the engine is increased and engine output is lowered. Remove the muffler baffle pipe periodically and clean off the carbon.

When the muffler connector at the muffler/exhaust pipe joint is worn, exhaust gases will leak. Replace a worn muffler connector with a new one.

Some riders remove muffler baffle pipes so their motorcycles will make more exhaust noise. With a two-cycle engine, however, the muffler baffle pipe not only silences engine exhaust noise but also prevents the blow-by of fuel mixture. Running without the muffler baffle pipes installed reduces engine output.

## 5. Dual Seat

Use a 10 mm wrench to remove two nuts fastening the dual seat to the fitting bracket. Pull the seat toward the rear of the motorcycle and remove it from the seat mounting boss at the rear of the fuel tank and the dual seat can be removed.

The dual seat fitting bracket is fitted to the frame with two $8 \times 18$ mm bolts.

**Fig. 89**
DUAL SEAT REMOVED FROM FRAME

## 6. Fuel Tank and Fuel Cock

The fuel tank is fitted to the frame with four bolts. Rubber shock dampers are installed on the mounting bolts to prevent vibration. The fuel tank holds 10 liters (2.64 US gal) of fuel including a reserve of 2 liters (0.53 US gal). A fuel cock and strainer is fitted under the left side of the fuel tank.

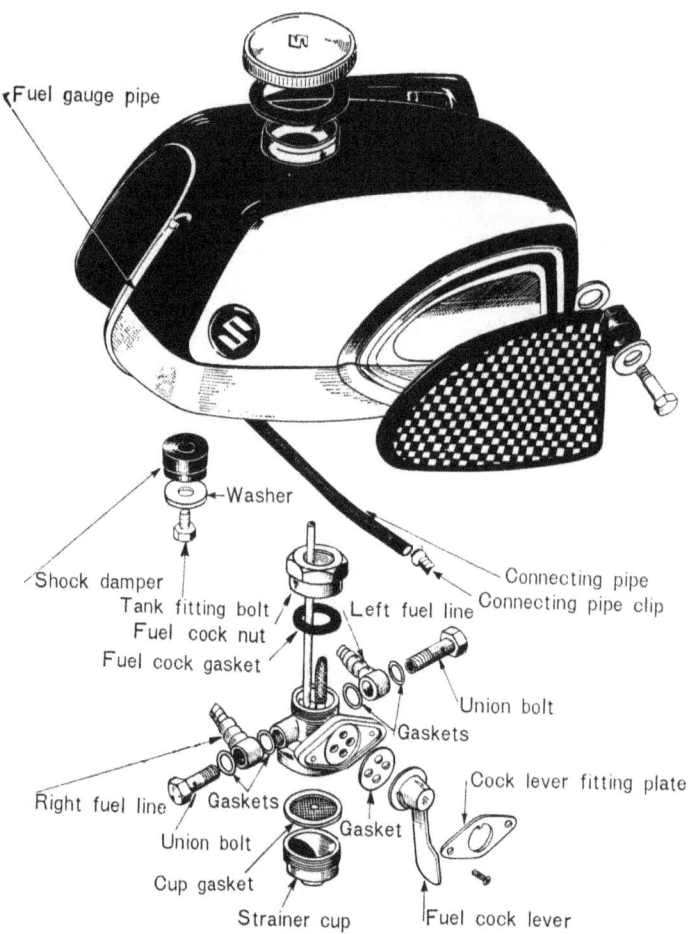

**Fig. 90**

FUEL TANK AND COCK

## A. Removing

Remove the dual seat first. Disconnect the fuel lines at the carburetors and drain the fuel from the tank. Disconnect the fuel tank connecting pipe. Remove the four mounting bolts and the fuel tank can be removed from the frame.

The fuel cock assembly can be removed from the tank by loosening the fuel cock nut.

## B. Inspecting and Servicing

If the fuel line, fuel gauge pipe, fuel tank connecting pipe, etc., are damaged and fuel leaks, replace with new parts.

If fuel leaks from joints, replace the gaskets with new ones.

Dirt or lint in the fuel system clogs the fuel line. Wash clean with gasoline before assembling.

If the fuel tank cap air vent is clogged, clean with compressed air or replace with a new one.

**Fig. 91**

REMOVING FUEL TANK

# 7. Speedometer

The magnet type speedometer on the T10 is simple in construction and responds sensitively without being affected by vibrations.

The speedometer has two main parts, the speed indicator which consists of a turning magnet, induction plate on which the shaft and needle are installed, hair spring which controls the turning of the induction plate and anti-magnetic cover, and the distance meter consisting of integrator rings and gears.

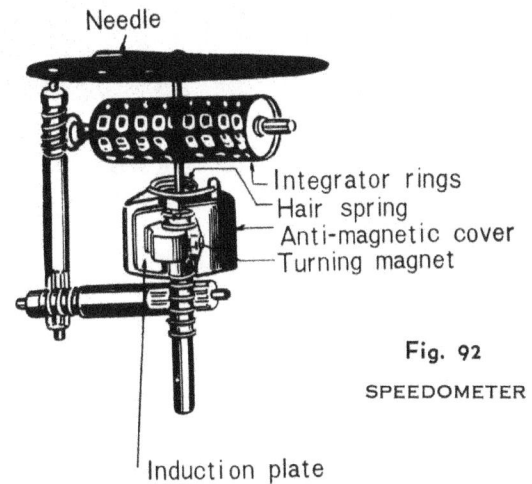

**Fig. 92**
SPEEDOMETER

## A. Speed Indicator

The speedometer needle mounted on the induction plate indicates the speed of the motorcycle when the induction plate turns according to the speed at which the magnet turns. When the motorcycle drive shaft turns, its revolutions are transmitted to turn the magnet through the speedometer gears and speedometer cable.

As the speed of the motorcycle increases, the speed of the rotation of the magnet increases and the induction plate which surrounds the magnet is moved in the same direction as the turning magnet by magnetic force. The turning of the induction plate is in proportion to the turning speed of the magnet.

The induction plate movement is stopped when its torque equals the hair spring tension, and the needle on the speedometer face, which is connected to the induction plate, indicates the speed of the motorcycle.

Do not tamper with the speedometer assembly as an improper hair spring adversely affects the operation of the speedometer. If the speedometer does not work correctly, replace with a new one.

## B. Distance Meter

The distance the motorcycle runs is indicated by the distance meter, which is turned through a set of gears by the speedometer cable. As the speed of the speedometer cable turning is very high while the milage meter turns only once every one-tenth of a mile (100 meters in kph meters), the difference in speeds is so great that ordinary spur gears are too unwieldy to make the reduction. Three sets of worm gears are used to obtain a proper reduction ratio.

The smallest unit integrator ring (1/10th mile, or 100 meters in kph speedometers) is driven directly by the gear, and the next larger unit ring is moved one notch (1/10th of a turn) by it each time it makes a full turn. Each succeeding larger unit ring is moved by its neighbor in the same manner.

One full turn of the smallest unit integrator ring requires 2,250 turns of the cable (1,400 turns in a kph speedometer). When the the cable turns at 2,250 rpm it indicates the motorcycle is running at 60 mph.

CAUTION: If the speedometer is turned in the reverse direction to turn back the distance meter, the hair spring will be damaged and the speedometer ruined. Do not turn back the speedometer.

# 8. Hydraulic Brake

## A. Comparison of Mechanical and Hydraulic Brakes

(1) **Mechanical Brake**

The power exerted by the rider in depressing the brake pedal is transmitted mechanically in the order of brake pedal, brake rod, link, brake arm and cam to expand the brake shoes, so that the motorcycle stops.

(2) **Hydraulic Brake**

Whereas all power is transmitted mechanically in the mechanical brake, in the hydraulic brake the power is transmitted by brake oil. When the brake pedal is depressed, the power is converted to oil pressure in the master cylinder. This oil pressure is transmitted to the rear brake cylinder at the rear wheel through a rubber hose and the rear brake cylinder expands the brake shoes, so that the motorcycle stops.

## B. Master Cylinder

### (1) Construction

The hydraulic brake master cylinder converts mechanical power exerted in the depressing of the brake pedal into oil pressure which is transmitted to the rear brake cylinder instantly.

The master cylinder consists of master piston, master piston return spring, master piston valve, master outlet valve, master piston push rod, etc. The construction is simple.

**Fig. 93**
HYDRAULIC BRAKE MASTER CYLINDER

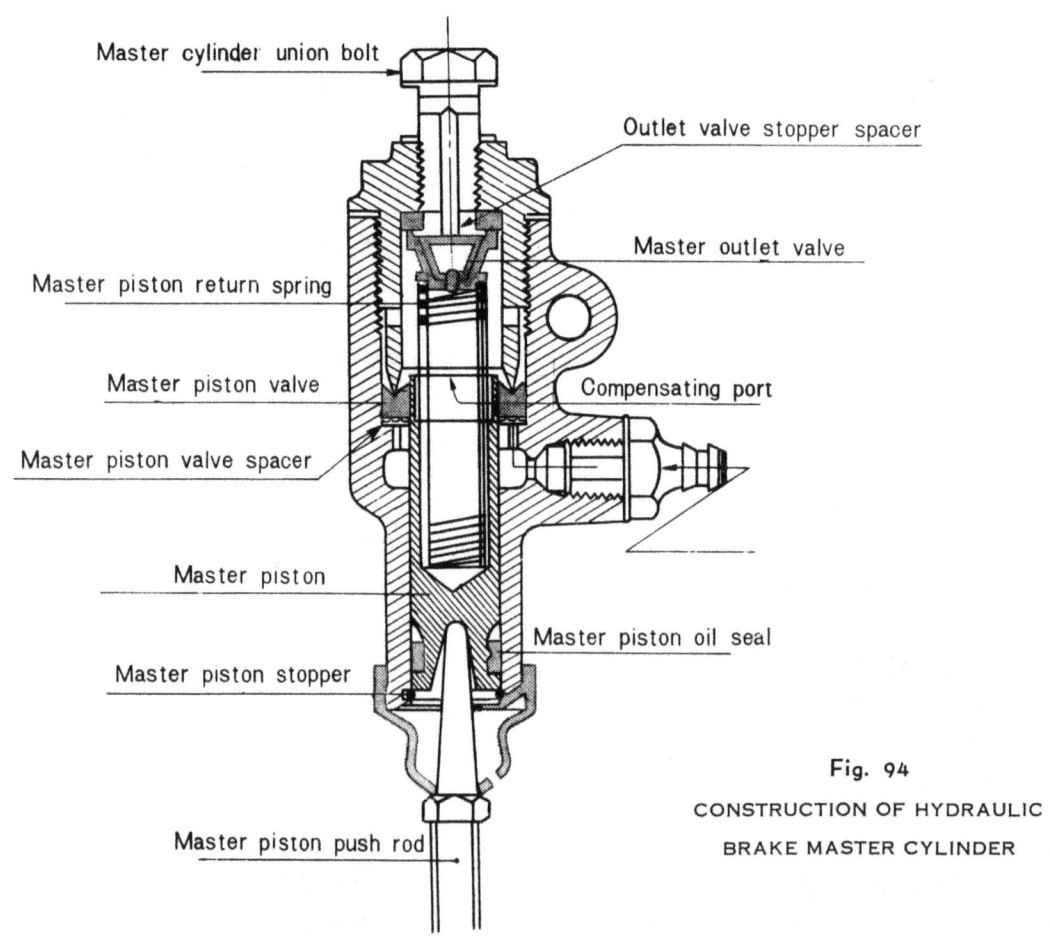

**Fig. 94**
CONSTRUCTION OF HYDRAULIC BRAKE MASTER CYLINDER

## (2) Operation

- When the brake pedal is depressed, the master piston push rod located at the rear end of the brake pedal pushes up the master piston. Most of the oil moved by the initial operation of the master piston flows back into the oil tank through the compensating port on the piston so that oil pressure is not generated in the master cylinder. If the master piston is moved with a rapid motion, however, a very small oil pressure is generated.

- As the piston moves further and the compensating port is closed when it passes the master piston valve, oil in the master cylinder cannot flow out and oil pressure is generated.

- Oil pushes the master outlet valve up and flows through the brake hose to the rear brake cylinder, as shown in the illustration.

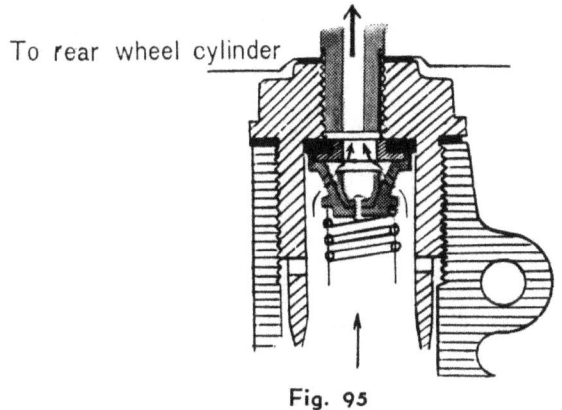

**Fig. 95**
OIL FLOWING TO REAR BRAKE CYLINDER

- This pressurized oil flows into the rear brake cylinder and pushes the rear brake cylinder pistons out by pressure on the oil seals. The pistons expand the brake shoes.

- When the brake pedal is released, the pedal is pulled back to its normal position by the brake pedal return spring. The master cylinder push rod ceases to push the master piston and the master piston is pushed back to its normal position by the master piston return spring.

- Brake oil in the rear brake cylinder flows back to the master cylinder through the brake hose.

- The brake shoes are pulled back to their normal positions by the brake shoe springs and push the rear brake pistons back to their normal positions.

- The master outlet valve will not open in a direction to allow the returning oil to enter the master cylinder. When oil pressure against the valve from the hose side is stronger than the master piston return spring, the returning oil pushes the master outlet valve down and enters the master cylinder through the gap between the master outlet valve and the master cylinder cap.

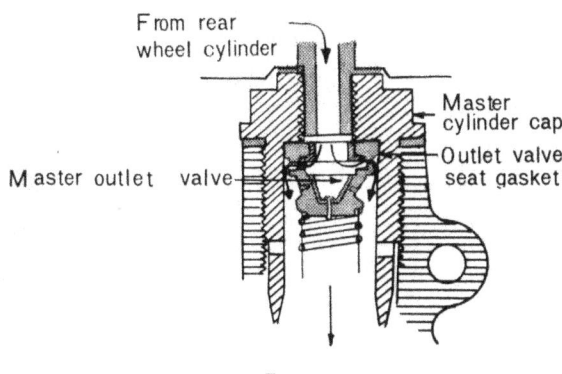

**Fig. 96**
OIL RETURNING TO MASTER CYLINDER

- When the strength of the oil pressure in the rear brake cylinder and the master piston return spring become the same, the master outlet valve seats on the master outlet valve seat gasket. A very slight residual pressure remains in the brake hose and rear brake cylinder.

- As the returning of oil from the rear brake cylinder is delayed slightly, a slight vacuum is produced in the master cylinder so that it is difficult for the master piston to return to its normal position rapidly. Oil in the brake oil tank flows into the master cylinder through the six cylinder oil intake ports and four cylinder cap holes pushing the master piston valve as shown in the illustration, and the vacuum is overcome. The piston returns to its normal position rapidly.

- When the compensating port on the master piston is uncovered, surplus oil in the master cylinder returns to the brake oil tank through the compensating port and conditions in the master cylinder return to normal.

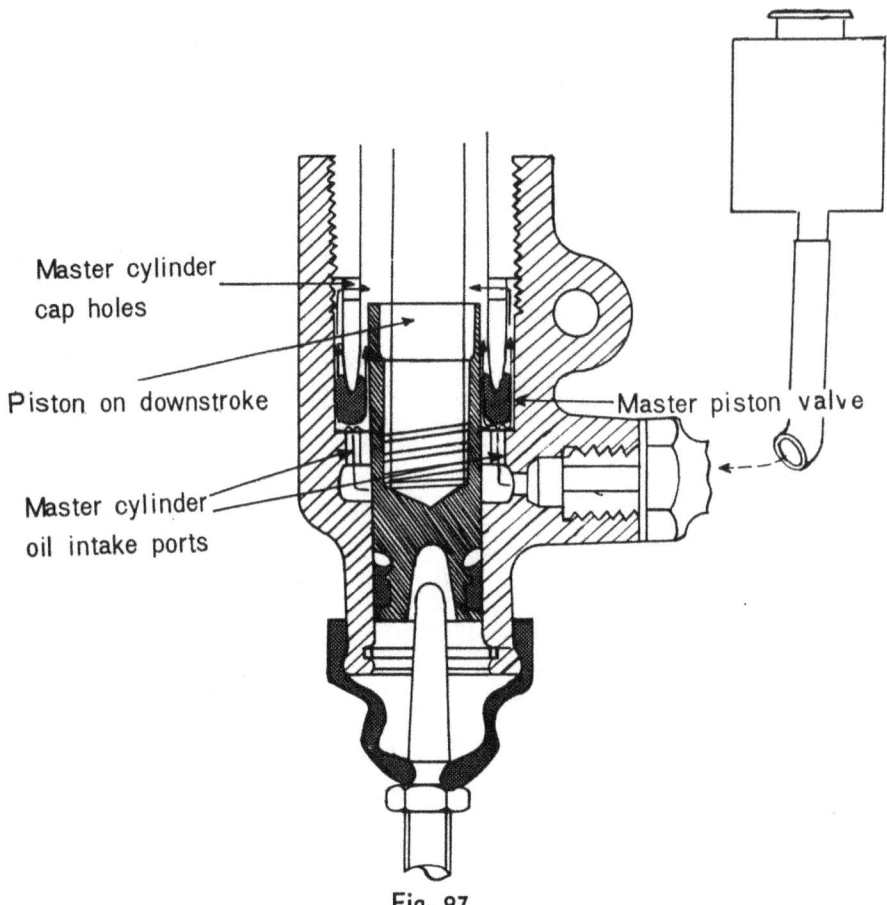

**Fig. 97**
MOMENTARY OIL FLOWING FROM BRAKE OIL TANK

### (3) Removing

- Remove the frame right cover.
- Bend the brake oil tank line closed in front of the master cylinder and tie it so that brake oil does not leak.
- Remove the brake oil tank line clip on the master cylinder brake oil line joint and pull the line off of the joint.
- Turn the master cylinder union bolt counter-clockwise with a 14 mm wrench and remove it. Remove the two union gaskets, one on top and one below the rear brake hose connection.
- Remove two master cylinder fitting bolts with a 12 mm wrench for the short 8 × 14 mm bolt inside the fender and a 14 mm wrench for the long 8 × 50 mm bolt outside the frame, and the 8 mm flat washers and lock washers. Pull the master cylinder upward and it can be removed.

### (4) Disassembling

- Remove the master cylinder assembly from the motorcycle, drain the brake oil out of it and wipe it clean with a rag.
- Pull off the master cylinder boot.
- Remove the master piston stopper with a small screw driver.
- Remove the master piston and master piston oil seal.
- Take out the master piston return spring.
- Clamp the master cylinder in a vise firmly at the installing bracket and remove the master cylinder cap with a 29 mm wrench. Remove the master cylinder cap gasket.
- Take out the master piston valve and master piston valve spacer.
- Remove the master outlet valve, master outlet valve stopper and master outlet valve seat gasket.

### (5) Tips on Handling

After the master cylinder is disassembled, wash all the parts with brake oil or cleaning solvent and dry with a clean rag.

CAUTION: If rubber parts such as the master piston valve, master piston oil seal, outlet valve seat gasket, etc., are washed with gasoline, they will be damaged. Never wash rubber parts with gasoline, kerosene, etc.

The master cylinder oil intake ports, master cylinder cap holes and master piston compensating port should be cleaned thoroughly.

Be careful not to damage parts when disassembling and assembling and do not allow them to get dirty.

Use only genuine Suzuki parts.

## (6) Tips on Assembling

- The brake will not work correctly if the master piston return spring is weak or shorter than standard or if a genuine part is not used.
- The brake will drag if the compensating port on the master piston is clogged.
- If the master piston stopper is not fitted in the proper position or is bent the master piston will be pushed up by it, closing the compensating port and causing the brake to drag.
- There should be a gap of approximately 0.5 mm (0.02 in) between the master piston and master piston push rod.
- Be sure to tighten the master cylinder union bolt and master cylinder cap tightly to prevent oil leaks.
- The 1 mm $\phi$ (0.04 in $\phi$) air vent on the master cylinder boot must be open. If the air vent is clogged, it will prevent the master piston from operating smoothly.
- Lubricate the master piston with brake oil before installing it.
- Always use genuine Suzuki gaskets.
- The brake pedal should be lubricated with grease so that it works easily and smoothly at all times.

## (7) Assembling

- Lubricate the master piston, master piston valve, outlet valve and outlet valve seat gasket with brake oil liberally.
- Install the master piston stopper in the groove in the lower part of the master cylinder.
- Clamp the cylinder in a vise and insert the master piston with the master piston oil seal installed on it into the master cylinder from the bottom.
- Install the master piston valve spacer.
- Insert the master piston valve.
- Install the master piston return spring inside the master piston.
- Fit the master outlet valve to the top of the master piston return spring.
- Fit the outlet valve seat gasket with the outlet valve spacer installed on it to the master outlet valve.
- Fit the master cylinder cap gasket and master cylinder cap. Tighten securely with a wrench.
- Install the master cylinder boot with the air vent on the back, that is the motorcycle side.

## (8) Installing

- Press the master piston push rod into the master cylinder boot and the hole on the master piston and attach the master cylinder to the frame with two bolts, flat washers and lock washers.
- Place gaskets on the top and bottom of the brake hose fitting and attach the brake hose to the master cylinder with the master cylinder union bolt.
- Fit the brake oil tank line to the master cylinder brake oil line joint and fasten with the brake oil line clip.
- Adjust the gap between the master piston push rod and the master piston to 0.5 mm (0.02 in).

(a) Loosen the push rod lock nut and screw the push rod in until it is separated from the master piston.

(b) Screw the push rod out gently until it touches the master piston lightly.

(c) Screw the push rod in $\frac{1}{4} \sim \frac{1}{2}$ of a turn and the gap between the push rod and master piston will be approximately 0.5 mm (0.02 in). Tighten the lock nut securely.

### (9) Inspection after Installation

Remove air from the brake system completely before adjusting the brake.

- Check to see that oil flows in the brake hose and brake oil tank line when the brake pedal is moved up and down. This can be checked while bleeding air from the brake system.

- When bleeding air, check to see that the master piston returns to its normal position without any trouble.

- Load the brake pedal with about 15 kg (33 lb) and check for oil leaks in the system, particularly at the master cylinder gaskets.

### (10) Adjustment and Maintenance Standards

( A )  Master Cylinder

- Check internal surfaces of master cylinder for rust or corrosion. Small areas of rust or corrosion can be repaired with fine emery paper. If serious rust or corrosion is found, replace with a new master cylinder.

- Check with a thin wire to make sure the hole in the brake oil line joint is not clogged.

- Check the six oil intake ports in the master cylinder with a thin wire to make sure they are not clogged.

- If the inside diameter of the master cylinder exceeds 15.123 mm (0.595 in), replace wtih a new one.

( B )  Master Cylinder Cap

- Check the master cylinder cap for small corrosion or damage to its taperd end in contact with the master piston valve, which can be repaired with fine emery paper, about ♯300.

NOTE: Damage on the rounded part on the end of the cylinder cap can damage the master piston valve, so if this part is seriously damaged replace with a new master cylinder cap.

If the threads of the master cylinder cap are damaged, replace the cap with a new one.

- Check the four oil holes in the master cylinder cap with a wire to make sure they are not clogged.

( C )  Master Piston

- Inspect the master piston for scratches, rust, corrosion, etc., and repair small defects with fine emery paper.

- If the defects are large or the compensating port or the section which fits the master piston oil seal is damaged, replace with a new master piston.

- Check the compensating port with a fine wire to make sure it is not clogged.

- If the clearance between the master piston and master cylinder wall exceeds 0.13 mm (0.00512in), replace the master piston. Standard clearance is 0.032 ~ 0.102 mm (0.00126 ~0.00402in).

( D )  Master Piston Valve and Oil Seal

If the valve or oil seal is damaged or stretched, replace with a new one. Replace the valve and oil seal every 10,000 km (6,000 miles).

( E )  Master Piston Valve Spacer

- Check the master piston valve spacer for cracks, bends or other damage and replace with a new one if any defect is found.

- File the outside of the spacer if it cannot be inserted into the master cylinder smoothly.

( F )  Master Piston Outlet Valve and Outlet Valve Seat Gasket

- Check for leaks by applying air pressure to the outlet valve from the brake hose side. Replace with a new valve if leaks are found.

- Replace damaged valve seat gasket. Parts made of rubber such as this gasket should be replaced every 10,000 km (6,000 miles).

( G )  Master Piston Return Spring

Check the master piston return spring for rust, breaks and other damage and replace if damaged or broken.

( H )  Master Cylinder Union Bolt

Replace if the threads are damaged or the head is damaged and the bolt cannot be tightened securely.

( I )  Master Piston Stopper

Place the master piston stopper on a flat surface to check if it is deformed or warped.

If it is bent over 0.1 mm (0.0039 in), repair or replace with a new stopper.

(J) Master Cylinder Cap Gasket and Union Gaskets

If the surfaces are rough or the gaskets are damaged and apt to leak oil, replace with new gaskets.

(K) Master Cylinder Boot

If the boot is damaged or worn, replace with a new one.

(L) Master Piston Push Rod

If the push rod is bent, repair or replace it with a new one. If the threads are damaged, replace with a new push rod.

## C. Rear Brake Cylinder

### (1) Construction

As shown in the illustration, the construction of the rear brake cylinder is very simple, consisting of oil seal spring, two oil seals and right and left pistons. The pistons are pushed out by oil pressure.

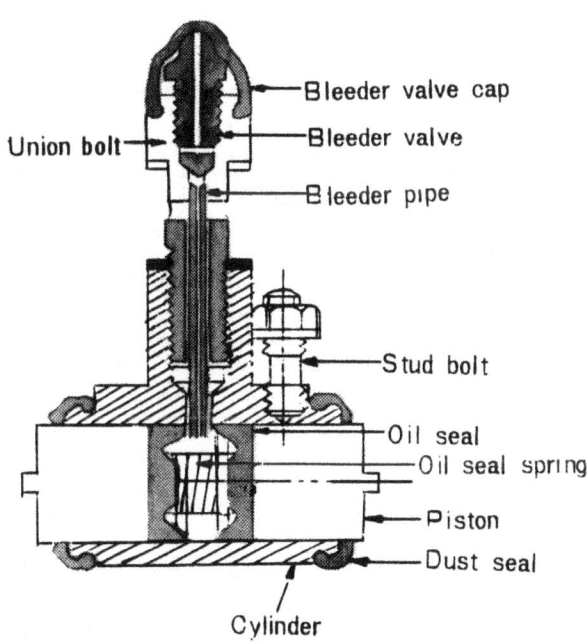

**Fig. 98**
CONSTRUCTION OF REAR BRAKE CYLINDER ASSEMBLY

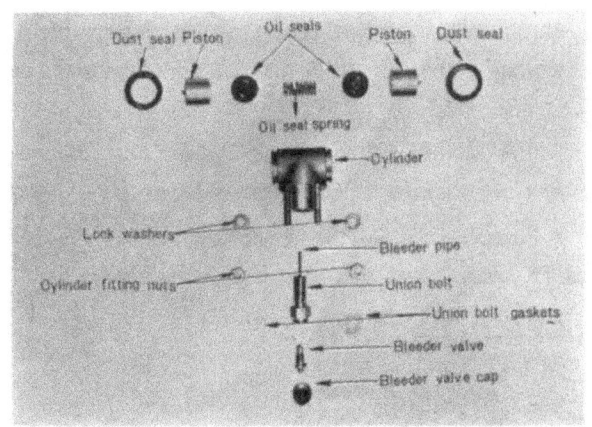

**Fig. 99**
DISASSEMBLED REAR BRAKE CYLINDER

### (2) Operation

- When the brake pedal is depressed, high pressure oil flows into the rear brake cylinder through the rear brake hose in the direction of the arrow in the illustration.

- This high pressure oil forces the oil seals to push out the pistons, which expand the brake shoes.

- When the brake pedal is released, the oil pressure decreases and the brake shoe return springs push the pistons back to their original position.

### (3) Tips on Handling

- Wash and service the components in the same manner as those of the master cylinder.

- Do not use anything other than a genuine spring for the rear brake cylinder.

- Be sure to install the rear brake cylinder spring in the cylinder in the center of the oil seals.

- Handle the rear brake cylinder bleeder pipe carefully.

CAUTION: When the bleeder pipe is bent or becomes short, replace with a new one.

- Do not tighten the bleeder valve excessively.

CAUTION: If the bleeder valve is tightened excessively, the end of the pipe will be damaged and it will be difficult to remove air from the brake oil.

- Lubricate the rear brake cylinder pistons with brake oil when installing them.

- Be sure to align the edges on the pistons

with the slots on the brake shoes when fitting the rear brake cylinder pistons and brake shoes. See Fig. 100.

CAUTION: If these are not aligned correctly, brake oil leakage will result.

• Remove air in the hydraulic brake system after assembling the rear brake cylinder.

Fig. 100
FITTING REAR BRAKE CYLINDER PISTON & BRAKE SHOE

### (4) Adjustment and Maintenance Standards

(A) Rear Brake Cylinder

• Check the inside of the rear brake cylinder for scratches, corrosion or rust. Small scratches and corrosion can be removed with fine emery paper. When defective parts cannot be repaired with emery paper, replace the cylinder with a new one.

• If inside diameter wear exceeds 0.08 mm (0.0032 in), replace the cylinder. Standard diameter is 18.5 mm (0.73 in).

• If a crack is found, replace the cylinder.

• Replace any damaged rear brake cylinder union bolt.

| Measurement | Standard | Clearance | | |
|---|---|---|---|---|
| | | Maximum | Minimum | Limit |
| Rear Brake Cylinder Inside Diameter | 18.5 mm (0.73 in) +0.033 mm (+0.0013 in) −0 | 0.086 mm (0.0034 in) | 0.020 mm (0.00079 in) | 0.15 mm (0.0059 in) |
| Rear Brake Piston Outside Diameter | 18.5 mm (0.73 in) −0.020 mm (−0.00079 in) −0.053 mm (−0.0021 in) | | | |

(B) Rear Brake Cylinder Piston

• If small scratches or corrosion is found on the piston surface, repair with fine emery paper. If defects are large, however, install a new piston.

• If the clearance between the rear brake cylinder and piston exceeds 0.15 mm (0.0059 in), replace both the cylinder and piston.

(C) Rear Brake Cylinder Oil Seals

Replace the oil seal when the edge of the lip is damaged or stretched. Replace the oil seal every 10,000 km (6,000 miles) even if no damage is evident.

(D) Rear Brake Cylinder Oil Seal Spring

Check to see if the spring is rusted. Replace with a new spring if there is considerable rust or its tension is decreased.

(E) Rear Brake Cylinder Dust Seal

Replace any damaged or defective dust seal.

(F) Rear Brake Cylinder Union Bolt

• Check to see if the oil channel in the bolt is clogged.

• Check to see if the bleeder valve threads are worn or damaged. Replace if necessary.

• Oil leaks if the cone part of the valve is worn. Replace a worn valve.

(G) Rear Brake Cylinder Bleeder Valve

• If the cone part of the valve is damaged, replace.

• Check to see if the valve hole is clogged.

• Replace if the threads are damaged.

(H) Rear Brake Cylinder Bleeder Pipe

If the bleeder pipe is clogged, clean it out with a wire.

(I) Rear Brake Cylinder Union Gaskets

Replace with a new one if the gasket is damaged.

(J) Bleeder Valve Cap

Replace with a new one if valve cap is damaged or defective.

### (5) Rear Brake Adjustment and Maintenance Standards

(A) Rear Hub Panel

• Check to see if the rear axle hole is loose. Replace if it is seriously loose.

• If the panel is cracked or the cam shaft hole is worn and the diameter is more than 0.2 mm (0.008 in) over the standard (12.0~12.1 mm, 4.72~4.76 in), replace with a new panel.

• If the rear axle hole is more than 0.1 mm (0.004 in) over the standard (17.0~17.043 mm, 6.69~6.71 in), replace with a new panel.

• If the panel warps and touches the rear hub, replace with a new panel.

(B) Brake Shoes

The wear limits of the brake lining are down to 0.5 mm (0.02 in) on the leading edge. Standard thickness of the brake lining is 3.6 mm (0.142 in).

(C) Rear Hub

• If a rear hub shock absorber has cracks or is worn, replace with a new one.

• If the inner surface of the hub is worn badly or ridged or the hub is warped, repair or replace.

• If there are cracks around the spoke fitting holes on the hub flange, replace with a new rear hub.

• If oil leaks from an oil seal, replace the oil seal. Replace oil seals every 20,000 km (12,000 miles) even if there is no leak.

(D) Brake Shoe Return Springs

• If the spring coils are stretched and the length seems to be excessive, replace with a new spring.

• If the spring is badly rusted or broken, replace with a new spring.

(E) Rear Brake Shoe Adjuster Cam Shaft

• If the clearance between the shaft and hub panel is more than 0.1 mm (0.0039 in), replace with a new cam shaft.

• If the serration is damaged badly and the rear brake shoe adjuster cam lever cannot be fitted, install a new cam shaft.

### (6) Tips on Installing Brake Hose

• Be careful not to twist brake hose when installing it. Fit it so that it does not touch the frame.

• Do not twist the brake hose when connecting it to the rear brake cylinder union bolt.

**Fig. 101**
BRAKE HOSE INSTALLATION

## D. Hydraulic Brake Oil

Suzuki Brake Oil, which is most highly recommended for use in the T10 hydraulic brake system, is a special high grade brake oil which fulfills the conditions listed below.

• Hydraulic brake oil must have chemical

stability and never solidify or corrode brake components such as pistons, cylinders, oil seals, brake hose, etc.

- The brake oil must resist vaporization and freezing.
- The brake oil boiling point must be at a high temperature so that the oil does not bubble even when it gets hot.
- The oil must not absorb water and must be unharmed by water.

Do not use anything other than genuine Suzuki Brake Oil in the T10 hydraulic brake system. Use only genuine Suzuki parts when replacing parts in the brake system.

All new motorcycles are filled with hydraulic brake oil when they are shipped and a 200 cc can of brake oil is attached to the motorcycle for adding to the brake system when needed.

The 200 cc can of brake oil is supplied through the regular parts channel.

| Part No. | Part Name | Remarks |
|---|---|---|
| T A 4385 | Brake Oil | 200 cc can |

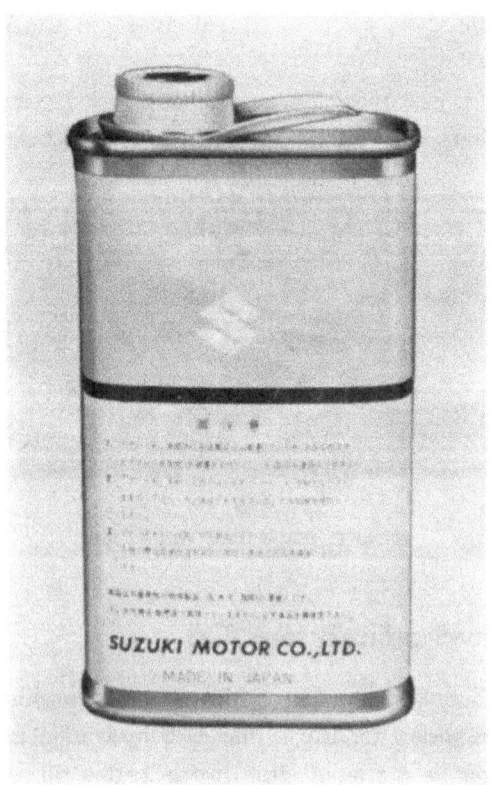

**Fig. 102**
BRAKE OIL

(1) **Tips on Handling**

Do not use brake oil which has been left standing in an open can. Always replace the lid on the can when brake oil is being kept for later use.

(2) **New Motorcycle Service**

- An air vent in the brake oil tank cap is not opened. Drill an air vent 2 mm (0.08 in) in diameter in the center of the brake oil tank cap, as shown in the illustration, before trying to adjust the brake.
- Check to see that the brake oil tank contains a sufficient amount of brake oil. If the oil level is low, add brake oil until the level is above the level line.
- Adjust the brake.

NOTE: If the air vent is not opened on the brake oil tank cap:

△ The brake does not work efficiently.
△ The brake drags.

If the oil level in the tank is low:

△ Air is apt to be inhaled into the system.
△ If the level is extremely low, brake operation becomes bad.

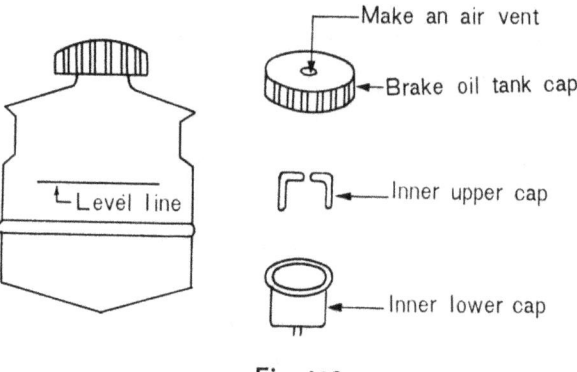

**Fig. 103**
BRAKE OIL TANK

## E. Adjusting Hydraulic Brake

(1) **Adjusting Rear Brake Shoe Clearance**

Turn screw A in the illustration clockwise until the brake lining contacts the rear hub wall. Turning the screw counterclockwise 1~2 turns, adjust the brake until the rear wheel turns freely. Check by spinning the wheel by hand.

Fig. 104
ADJUSTING REAR BRAKE SHOE CLEARANCE

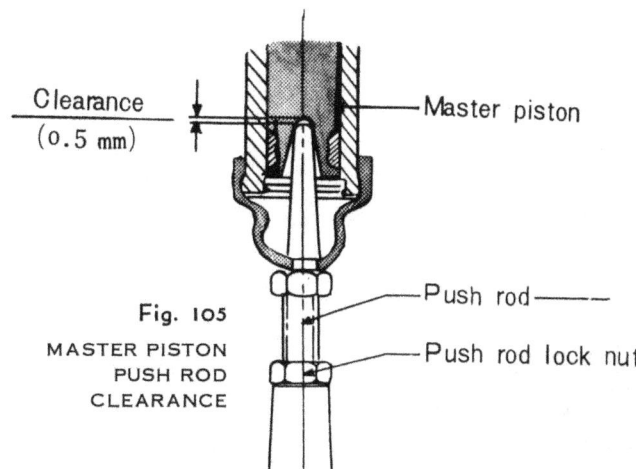

Fig. 105
MASTER PISTON PUSH ROD CLEARANCE

## (2) Adjusting Brake Pedal Play

Play in the brake pedal can be adjusted by changing the gap between the master piston push rod and the master piston inside the master cylinder. Loosen the push rod lock nut with a 10 mm wrench, turn the push rod to the right and left and check the play by depressing the brake pedal lightly. There should be 2~3 mm (0.08~0.12 in) of play in the brake pedal before the push rod touches the master piston. Tighten the push rod lock nut firmly after adjusting. Then the clearance between the push rod and master piston is approximately 0.5 mm (0.02 in), which is standard.

CAUTION: If there is no play in the brake pedal, the brake is engaged at all times. Be sure to adjust the play properly. Play in the brake pedal should be vertical. There should be no axial play in the brake pedal.

## (3) Clearance between Push Rod and Master Piston

Adjusting play in the brake pedal adjusts the clearance between the push rod and master piston, as explained in the preceding section.

It is most important that there should be a clearance between the push rod and the master piston. Standard gap is 0.5 mm (0.02 in).

If the push rod is always pushing the master piston up, the compensating port is closed, closing the channel between the master cylinder and the brake oil tank. When the brake pedal is depressed frequently, oil flows into the cylinder from the brake oil tank but the brake oil cannot return to the oil tank so that pressure in the master cylinder increases. Finally there will be no travel in the brake pedal and the brake will be completely engaged and seized.

## (4) Removing Air from Hydraulic Brake System

Remove air from the hydraulic brake system when adjusting the brake, when changing brake oil and after disassembling and inspecting brake system.

• Fill the brake oil tank with brake oil.
• Remove the rubber bleeder valve cap and depress the brake pedal several times by hand.
• Turn the bleeder valve out 1~2 turns with a 9 mm wrench. Air will be expelled first before brake oil flows out. Tighten the bleeder valve again to increase the pressure in the brake system.
• Repeat the same procedures again and again and air foam mixed with oil will be expelled, then gradually only brake oil will flow out. When only oil blows out vigorously, tighten the bleeder valve firmly. The air bleeding process is complete.

CAUTION: Do not tighten the bleeder valve excessively or the tip of the valve and the bleeder pipe end will be damaged and brake oil will leak.

Attach a vinyl pipe to the bleeder valve or

cover the valve with a rag to absorb the brake oil and prevent the oil from getting into the hub drum.

After removing air from the brake system, depress the brake pedal strongly and check to see if oil leaks from the master cylinder, rear brake cylinder or brake hose.

Wipe all parts clean with a dry rag.

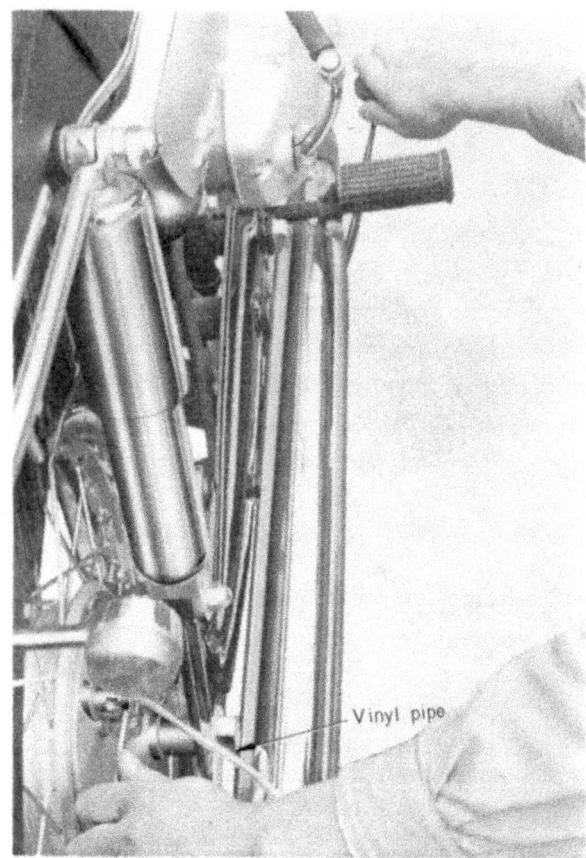

**Fig. 106**
REMOVING AIR FROM HYDRAULIC BRAKE

### (5) Changing Brake Oil

Change the hydraulic brake oil every 10,000 km (6,000 miles).

Loosen the bleeder valve and drain the brake oil until only a small amount remains in the oil tank. Fill the brake oil tank with genuine Suzuki Brake Oil and follow the procedure for bleeding air out of the system listed in the preceding section.

CAUTION: When replacing oil, the old oil remaining in the brake system will be expelled first and then air bubbles will be exhausted, so do not stop the bleeding operation when the old oil begins to come out.

## F. Daily Inspection

• Always check to see that the brake system is in good condition before riding the motorcycle.

• Check to see that the brake hose and connections are coupled correctly and check for brake oil leaks.

## G. Periodic Inspection

• Adjust the brake every 500 km (300 miles) and check the amount of oil in the brake oil tank.

• Lubricate the brake pedal with grease every 5,000 km (3,000 miles) and check to see that the pedal moves smoothly.

• Inspect the rear wheel hub after the first 500 km (300 miles) and every 3,000 km (1,900 miles) afterward.

• Replace the brake oil every 10,000 km (6,000 miles).

• Disassemble and inspect the hydraulic brake system every 10,000 km (6,000 miles). Replace the oil seals when the brake is disassembled.

### (1) Tips on Periodic Inspection

• Remove the rear hub panel and operate the brake pedal. Check to see that the brake shoes return to their original positions smoothly. If the returning operation is bad, replace the rear brake cylinder side brake shoe return spring.

• Check to see that the brake oil channel in the hose, master cylinder and rear brake cylinder is not clogged.

• Tighten brake hose connections firmly to prevent oil leaks.

• If the rear brake cylinder dust seal is damaged, replace it with a new one.

## H. Hydraulic Brake Trouble Causes and Repairs

### (1) If Rear Brake Drags

• The master cylinder compensating port is clogged.

Disassemble the master cylinder and clean the compensating port with a wire.

- The brake shoes do not return to their normal positions because of defective operation of the master cylinder.

Check to see if the master piston valve is stretched. If the master piston valve is defective, replace with a new one.

Cracks and scratches on the master piston can cause poor return of the rear brake shoes. Replace with a new master piston.

- The master piston push rod is pushing the master piston all the time.

Adjust the gap between the master piston and push rod to 0.5 mm (0.02 in).

- Brake shoes are improperly adjusted.

Turning the wheel by hand lightly, check to see if the brake shoes are dragging against the drum.
Adjust with the rear brake shoe adjuster.

- Brake hose connection is clogged.

Loosen the union bolt and depress the brake pedal gently to see if brake oil flows out. If the system is clogged, clean it.

- The brake shoe return spring is damaged.

Inspect the spring. If spring is worn or damaged, replace it with a new one.

- Rear brake cylinder pistons do not move smoothly.

Check the pistons and cylinder for rust, and repair with fine emery paper.

- Brake shoe positioning bolt touches the brake shoe and obstructs its return.

The brake shoe is not installed properly or the positioning bolt is bent. Correct the shoe mounting or straighten the bolt.

### (2) Insufficient Braking and Large Brake Pedal Travel

- Brake lining is worn or brake improperly adjusted.

The standard thickness of the brake lining is 3.6 mm (0.142 in). When the leading edge of the lining is worn to 0.5 mm (0.02 in), replace the brake shoe.

- Oil leaks from the hose connections or the middle of the brake hose.

Tighten connections firmly, replace gaskets or replace hose.

- Air is mixed with oil in the brake system. Bleed the air out completely.
- Amount of oil in the brake oil tank is low.

Add brake oil to above level line. Bleed air from the brake system completely.

- Master piston valve is stretched and not fitting against the cylinder properly.

Fit a new master piston valve.

- Oil leaks from rear brake cylinder oil seals.

Check to see that the rear brake cylinder spring is fitted in the center of the oil seals. Replace worn or damaged oil seal.

- Gasoline is in brake oil.

Drain the brake oil completely and replace with fresh genuine Suzuki Brake Oil.

NOTE: Adjust the brake after correcting these troubles.

### (3) Abnormal Noise in Brake

- The panel is warped and the lining does not contact the drum squarely.

Replace panel with new one.

- Some part which is not supposed to touch another is dragging.

Find the part which is out of position and repair it.

## I. Tips on Handling Hydraulic Brake

- Use only genuine Suzuki Brake Oil.
- Check the amount of oil in the brake oil tank and add if needed. Brake oil should be kept above the level line at all times.
- The maximum travel of the brake pedal is 80~85 mm (3.2~3.35 in). Adjust the brake before pedal travel become as large as 40 mm (1.58 in). Brake pedal travel should be 25~30 mm (1~1.2 in) after adjustment, If travel is excessive after adjustment, bleed air from he brcke system.
- Friction extremely shortens the life of the brake hose, which is made of rubber. Be sure that the brake hose does not touch or rub against any part of the motorcycle. Replace a worn brake hose.

## J. Removing Rear Wheel

Remove the torque link from the rear hub panel with a 17 mm wrench.

Straighten the cotter pin and pull it out. Remove the rear axle nut with a 23 mm wrench. It is better to remove the brake hose from the brake hose clip.

Strike the rear axle and pull it out from the hub panel side. Remove drive chain adjusters and rear axle spacer.

NOTE: Take care not to scratch the right muffler when removing the axle. Press down on the rear of the dual seat to depress the springs so that the axle does not hit the muffler.

It is not necessary to remove the sprocket mounting drum shaft nut.

Lean the motorcycle to the left and pull out the rear wheel with the rear hub panel in place until it is near the right muffler as shown in Fig. 108. The rear hub panel can be removed from the hub in this position and the wheel pulled from under the motorcycle.

**Fig. 108**
REMOVING REAR WHEEL FROM PANEL

**Fig. 107**
STRIKING OUT REAR AXLE NUT

## K. Inspection and Service

Check brake shoes and brake shoe springs for wear and replace with new parts if needed. The brake lining, should not be thinner than 0.5 mm (0.02 in) on the leading edge. The standard thickness of the lining is 3.6 mm (0.14 in).

If the rear brake oil seals are worn, brake oil leaks and performance of the brake is bad. Replace worn oil seals immediately.

Check the brake hose for cracks and replace with a new one if any cracks or leaks are found.

Do not allow rear wheel parts to get dirty while they are disassembled. Wash with cleaning solvent before reassembling. Never use gasoline or similar fluids for washing parts, as they adversely affect parts made of rubber. Dry all parts with a clean rag. Clean the internal surface of the hub drum with fine emery paper.

Check the rear brake shoe adjuster cam shaft for rust and polish with emery paper if needed. If the cam shaft is rusted in the rear hub panel, remove it by striking with a hammer. Lubricate the cam shaft for smooth operation before reassembling rear wheel.

Check rear hub shock absorbers for cracks or other damage and replace if needed. Check the fitting screws and make sure they are tight.

Check bearings and oil seals for damage or wear and replace if necessary.

Be sure to bleed air from the hydraulic brake system after fitting the wheel. See Hydraulic Brake section.

# 9. Front Brake

## A. Disassembling

| Operation | Part No. | Part Name | Q'ty | Tools | Remarks |
|---|---|---|---|---|---|
| Remove Front Axle | N K 162 F | front axle nut | 1 | 23 mm wrench | |
| | A A H 1491 | front axle washer | 1 | | place heavy block under engine to raise front wheel, see Fig. 109 |
| | A A B 2364 | brake rod adjusting nut | 1 | | |
| | A A B 2363 | brake cam lever pin | 1 | | |
| | A A B 2362 | brake rod adjusting spring | 1 | | |
| | T B 5751-7 | brake cable boot | 1 | | |
| | S B 5451 | front axle | 1 | wooden hammer | striking with hammer, pull out on left side |
| Remove Wheel | | | | | |
| Remove Front Hub Panel From Wheel | | | | | |
| Remove Brake Shoes | T B 5431 | brake shoe | 2 | | see Fig. 110 |
| | A A H 1261 | brake shoe spring | 2 | | |

Fig. 109
REMOVING FRONT WHEEL

Fig. 110
REMOVING BRAKE SHOES FROM PANEL

After disassembling, check to see if brake shoe springs are worn. Replace with new ones if necessary. Remove the brake cam shaft and check it for rust. If the cam is rusted or does not move smoothly, polish it with emery paper and apply a small amount of grease.

## B. Assembling

To assemble, insert the ends of the brake shoe springs in the holes on the brake shoes with the ends of the springs on the front hub panel side. See Fig. 111. Expand the brake shoes and install on the panel.

Fit the front wheel to the fork in the reverse order from disassembling.

Standard tightening torque of the front axle nut is 600 kg-cm (520 lb-in).

Fig. 111  BRAKE SHOE SPRING ENDS DIRECTION

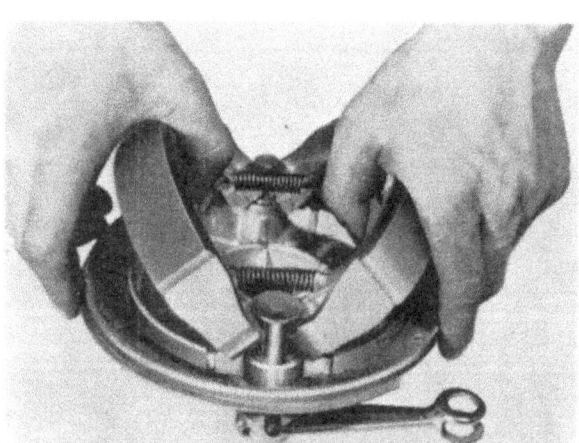

Fig. 112  INSTALLING BRAKE SHOES

Fig. 113  TIGHTENING FRONT AXLE NUT

## C. Brake Drum and Brake Lining

If the brake drum is ridged or worn, the brake lever travel increases and braking is delayed. If it is considerably worn, the brake cam shaft will turn 90° when the brake applied and cannot return to its normal position, locking the brake. Replace the hub drum.

The brake lining should not be thinner than 0.5 mm (0.02 in) on the leading edge. Standard thickness is 3.6 mm (0.14 in).

## D. Inspecting and Replacing Wheel Bearings and Hub Drum Oil Seals

Remove the oil seals on both sides with an oil seal puller. See Fig. 114.

To remove the bearings, place a rod against the bearing as shown in the illustration and strike the rod with a hammer from the opposite side.

An oil seal with a damaged lip cannot work correctly and dust and dirt get into the hub drum and grease leaks out. Wear of the bearings is hastened and grease in the drum can cause the brake to slip. Replace the oil seal if the lip is damaged.

Replace oil seals every 20,000 km (12,000 miles) even if no damage is evident.

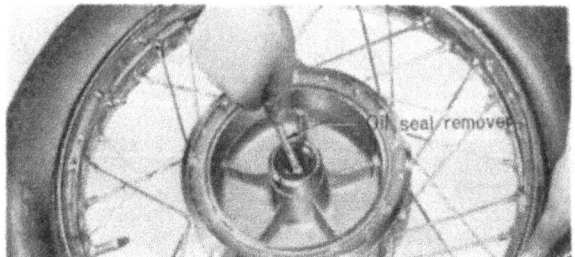

Fig. 114  REMOVING HUB DRUM OIL SEAL

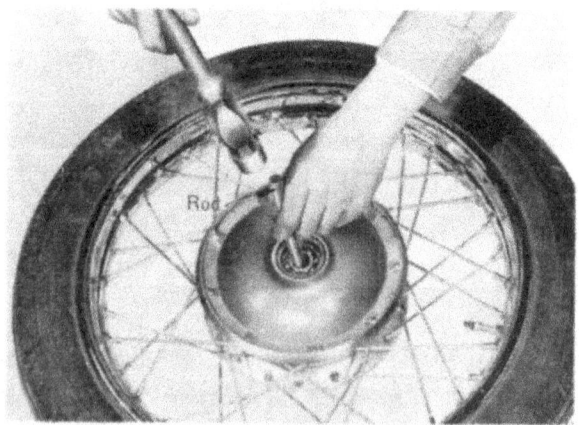

Fig. 115  REMOVING HUB DRUM BEARING

(1) **Tips on Installing Bearings**

Pack the steel balls in grease before pressing the bearings into the wheel hub.

Do not strike the bearing inner race.

Install the bearing with the stamped surface facing the outside.

Use a special tool to install bearings.

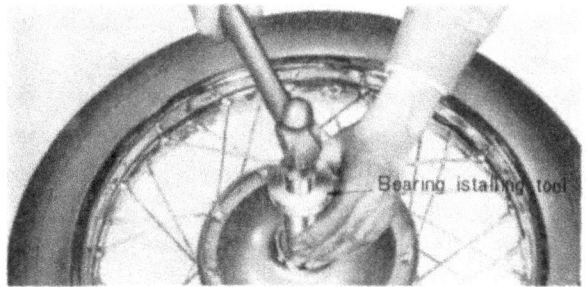

Fig. 116
INSTALLING HUB DRUM BEARING

(2) **Inspecting Bearings**

Even slight damage or play in bearings will hasten their wear and the bearing temperature will rise, causing the bearing to seize.

Check the bearings carefully.

Wash the bearing with cleaning solvent before inspecting. Hold the bearing by the inner race with a finger, as shown in Fig. 117.

Turn the outer race with a finger and check to see that the outer race turns smoothly. If the outer race does not turn lightly, quietly and smoothly, or if noise is heard, the bearing is defective and must be replaced with a new one.

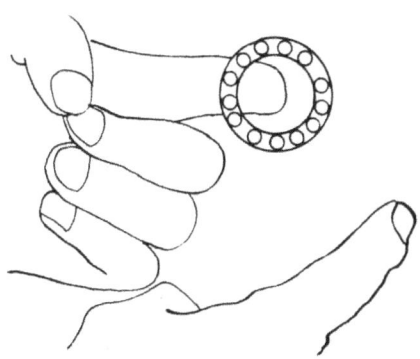

Fig. 117
CHECKING BALL BEARING

# 10. Inspecting Rim Shake

Inspect front and rear wheel rim shake with a dial gauge as shown in the illustration. If the rim shakes over 5 mm (0.2 in), retighten the spokes. Wheel rim shake should be less than 3 mm (0.116 in). If rim shake cannot be corrected by retightening the spokes, replace the rim with a new one.

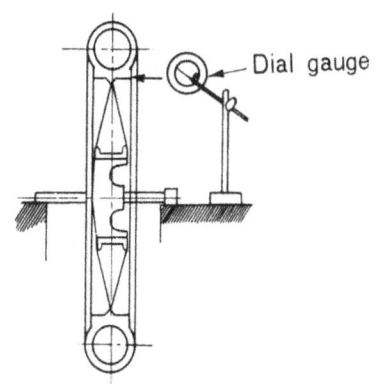

Fig. 118
INSPECTING RIM SHAKE

# 11. Wheel Alignment

Check wheel alignment as shown in Fig. 119. If the wheels are not aligned properly, correct with drive chain adjusters. If it can't be corrected with them, check the frame, front fork, rear swinging arm and rims for deformity and warping. Replace any defective part.

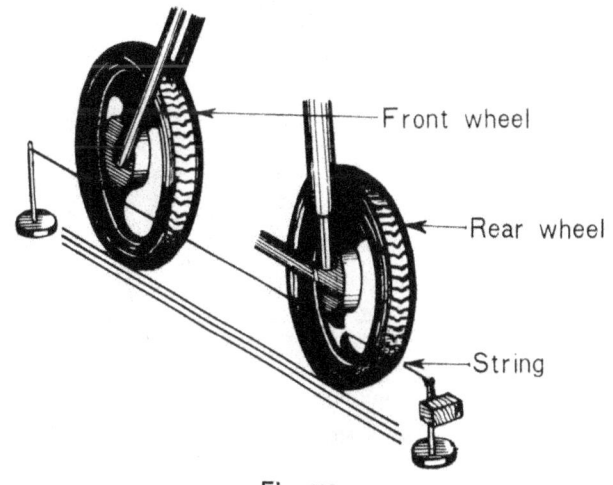

Fig. 119
INSPECTING WHEEL ALIGNMENT

# 12. Front Fork

## A. Disassembling

Remove the front wheel. See "Disassembling Front Brake" section.

Drain fork oil by removing drain plugs on bottom of fork legs.

Remove front fender brace bolts with a 12 mm wrench. Take care not to scratch the fender when removing it from between the fork legs.

Loosen the four handlebar fitting bolts with a 10 mm socket wrench and lay the handlebar on the fuel tank. Place a thick cloth on the tank first to keep it from being scratched by the handlebar. See Fig. 120.

Remove the fork fitting bolts with a 17 mm wrench.

Loosen the steering stem pinch bolts with a 17 mm wrench. It is not necessary to remove the bolts.

Pull the fork leg out. See Fig. 121. Pour fork oil out of the fork from the fork fitting bolt hole if it was not drained earlier.

**Fig. 120**
HANDLEBAR LAID ON FUEL TANK

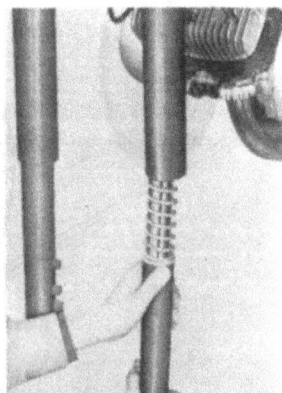

**Fig. 121**
REMOVING FORK LEG

Remove the spring from the fork inner tube. Clamp the inner tube in a vise and turn the outer tube while pulling it toward the bottom of the fork leg. Turn until the slot in the fork inner tube guide fits the stopper on the inner tube, when a click can be heard. Unscrew the outer tube by turning it to the left.

CAUTION: Wrap a strip of rubber around the upper end of the inner tube when clamping it in the vise so the inner tube is not marred or damaged. See the illustration.

Do not use the front axle as a tool to turn the outer tube and unscrew it from the inner tube. Remove the fork oil seal, fork oil seal seat and fork inner tube guide.

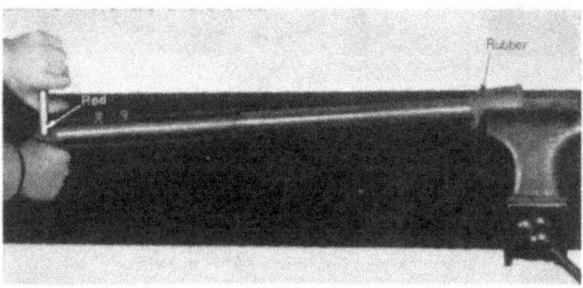

**Fig. 122**
REMOVING FORK INNER TUBE FROM OUTER TUBE

**Fig. 123**
DIASSEMBLED FORK LEG

## B. Inspection and Servicing

• If oil seals are worn or damaged, damping performance is lowered, noise is produced and oil leaks. Replace damaged or worn oil seals with new ones.

• Check the inner tube for scratches on its surface, correct with fine emery paper if scratches are found.

• If the inner tube has been bent, it is not necessary to replace with a new part if the old inner tube can be straightened with a press.

## C. Assembling

Wash all parts with cleaning solvent and dry with a clean rag.

Assemble the front fork by reversing the steps for disassembly, but pay particular attention to the following points.

Be careful not to damage the lip of the oil seal when installing it. Slip a piece of vinyl, etc., over the top of the inner tube when installing the oil seal to prevent damage to the lip of the oil seal. See Fig. 124.

Take care not to scratch or score the inner tube. A scratched inner tube sliding surface produces rough damping action.

Lubricate the outer tube with oil when installing the oil seal so it can be fitted easily. Press the oil seal into place gently, taking care not to damage it. A socket wrench or pipe may be used to press on the oil seal. See Fig. 125.

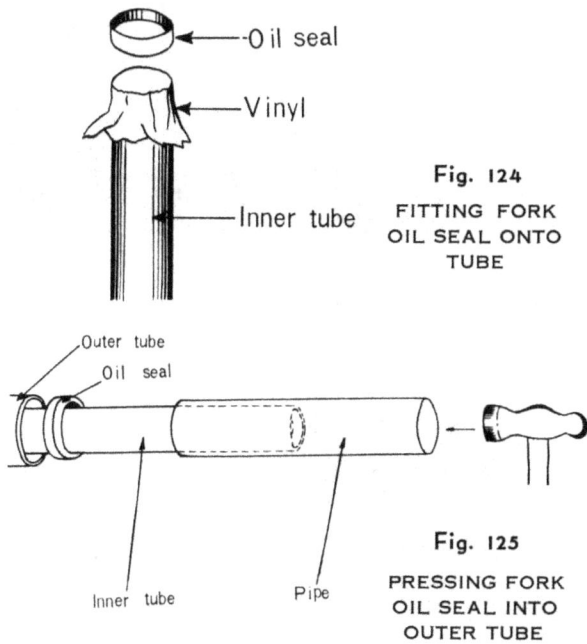

Fig. 124 FITTING FORK OIL SEAL ONTO TUBE

Fig. 125 PRESSING FORK OIL SEAL INTO OUTER TUBE

Fill each fork leg with 230 cc (0.49 US pt) of oil. Use a mixture of 6 parts of #30 motor oil to 4 parts of #60 spindle oil. Pour the oil through the hole in the top of the tube.

If the fork holds the proper amount of oil, the oil level is 370 mm (14.6 in) from the fork fitting bolt hole when the motorcycle is placed on the center stand.

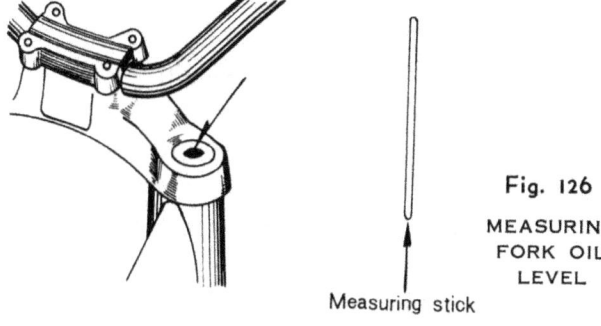

Fig. 126 MEASURING FORK OIL LEVEL

The flat side of the fork spring cover guide must be aligned with the welded part inside the outer cover when assembling.

Fit the stopper on the inner tube to the groove in the fork inner tube guide and pull the inner tube up with a front fork assembling tool with the fender brace bolt holes on the outer tube facing forward. Temporarily tighten the pinch bolt.

Push the outer tube up and release the inner tube stopper from the fork inner tube guide groove. Turn the outer tube 90° toward the inside. See Fig. 128.

Check to see that the fork inner tube shock damper is installed. If it is not, fork oil will leak. Tighten the fork fitting bolt securely.

Fit the front wheel after installing the front fender. Tighten the pinch bolts after the front axle nut has been tightened.

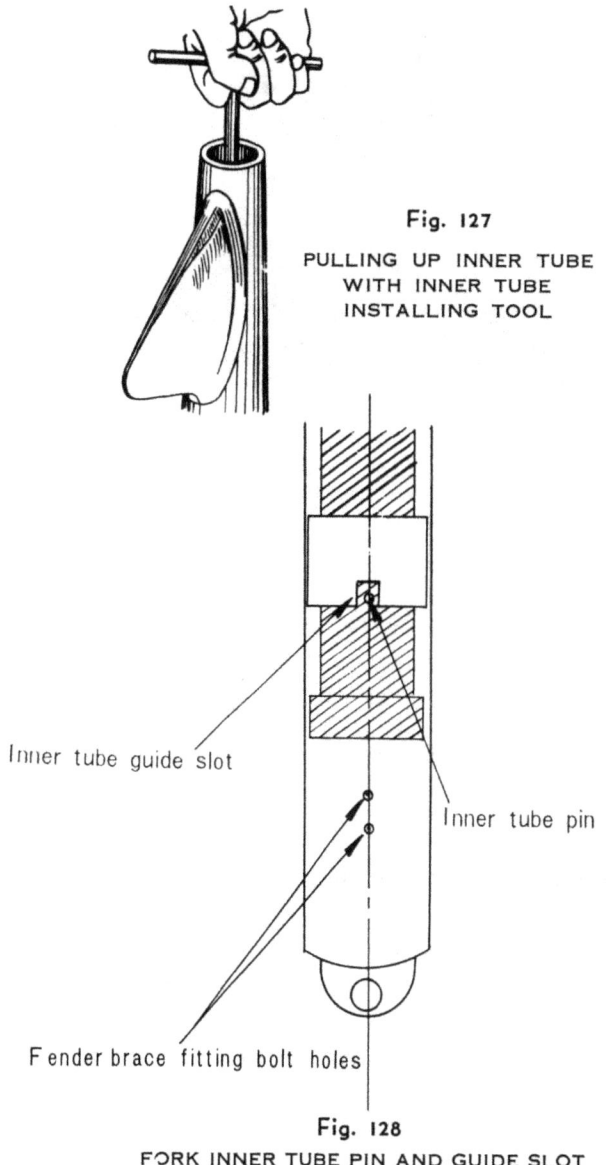

Fig. 127 PULLING UP INNER TUBE WITH INNER TUBE INSTALLING TOOL

Fig. 128 FORK INNER TUBE PIN AND GUIDE SLOT

# 13. Steering Stem

## A. Disassembling

It is better to remove the front wheel and front fender first. Disconnect the wiring harnesses from the right and left switches inside the head lamp housing.

Remove the throttle cable, brake cable and clutch cable from the handlebar.

Remove the handlebar damper adjusting knob, knob stopper, adjusting spring cover, adjusting spring and adjusting spring seat.

Take off the handlebar clamp by removing 4 fitting bolts with a 10 mm wrench and remove the handlebar.

Fig. 130
REMOVING STEERING STEM HEAD WITH HAMMER

Fig. 129
HANDLEBAR WITH CABLES AND WIRES DISCONNECTED

Remove both fork fitting bolts.

Use a 23 mm wrench to remove the steering stem head nut and a hammer if necessary to remove the head.

Remove the steering stem lock nut with a small steering stem nut wrench.

Remove the steering stem nut with a large steering stem nut wrench.

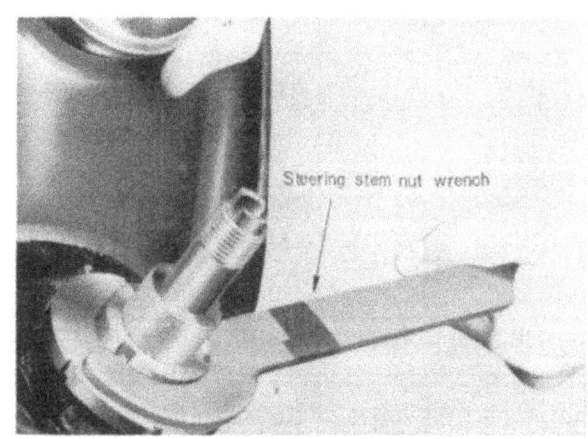

Fig. 131
LOOSENING STEERING STEM LOCK NUT

Remove the upper race steel balls. Be careful not to drop them. There are 18 steel balls each in the steering upper and lower races.

Place a heavy block under the engine and raise the front of the motorcycle.

Remove the steering stem with the front fork installed. Be careful not to drop the lower race steel balls or otherwise damage the fork or steering stem.

Remove the lower race steel balls.

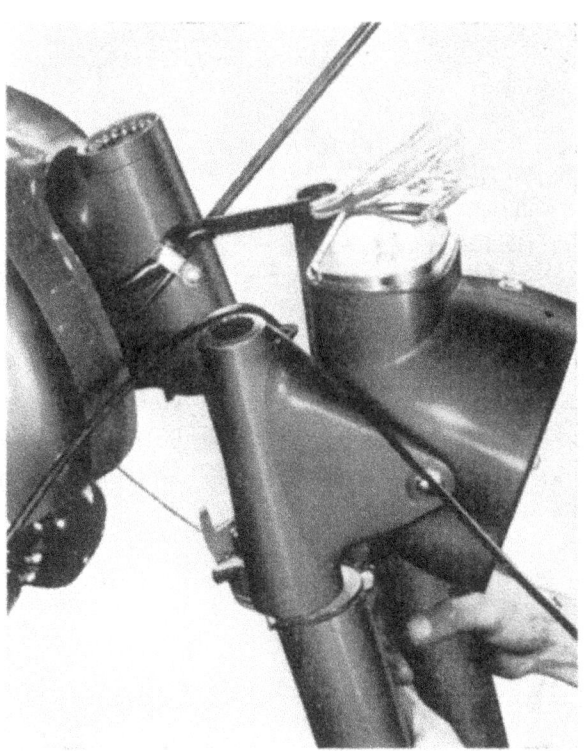

**Fig. 132**
REMOVING STEERING STEM
WITH FRONT FORK INSTALLED

## B. Inspection and Servicing

Check the steel balls and bearing races for wear or damage, or rust due to insufficient lubrication. A defective steering head steel ball causes dangerous, unsmooth steering. Replace worn or damaged parts with new ones.

## C. Assembling

The steering stem can be installed in the reverse order from disassembly, but take care on the following points.

Pack the steel ball bearings with grease.

Turn the steering stem nut with one hand until there is no play in the steering head, and then undo it $\frac{1}{4}$ of a turn. Tighten the steering stem lock nut firmly with a special tool.

# ELECTRICAL EQUIPMENT

## 1. Charging System

### A. Starter Dynamo

The T10 has a push button and starter dynamo starting system. The starter dynamo has two functions, as a starter for starting the engine and as a dynamo for charging the battery. When starting the engine, the starter dynamo works as an electric starter. After the engine is started the starter dynamo works as a dynamo to charge the battery. Contact breakers, timing advancer assembly, etc., are mounted on the starter dynamo, so that it also causes sparking in the cylinders.

The starter dynamo delivers strong torque when it works as an electric starter. It has eight field coils and incorporates a regulator and is a constant voltage dynamo when charging the battery.

### (1) Specifications

| | |
|---|---|
| Nominal output as starter | 0.26 kw |
| Nominal output as dynamo | 100 w |
| Turning Direction | counterclockwise viewed from dynamo side |
| Number of poles | 8 |
| Carbon brush length | 20 mm (0.788 in) |
| Air gap | 0.45 mm (0.0177 in) |
| Torque when engaged | 1.30 kg-m (9.39 ft-lb) |
| Current when engaged | 140 amperes or below |
| Voltage when engaged | 8 v |
| Rpm at normal temperature | 750 |
| Points gap | 0.3~0.4 mm (0.012~0.016 in) |
| Ignition timing | 7° before tdc (no advance)<br>30° before tdc (fully advanced) |
| Ignition timing advance begins at | 1,200 rpm |
| Ignition timing advance ends at | 1,500 rpm |
| Condenser capacity | 0.22 μF |
| Capacity as starter | more than 100 times at 5 second intervals at normal temperature |

### (2) Construction

The starter dynamo consists of a stator which is fixed on the crankcase and an armature which turns with the crankshaft.

Carbon brushes, contact breaker cam oil felts, contact point assemblies and condensers are fitted to the stator as shown in Fig. 133.

A large electric current flows when starting the engine, so four carbon brushes are fitted.

There are eight field coils inside the stator. Field coils for starter and for dynamo are incorporated in each coil.

The armature is fitted on the tapered end of the crankshaft with a key and keyway.

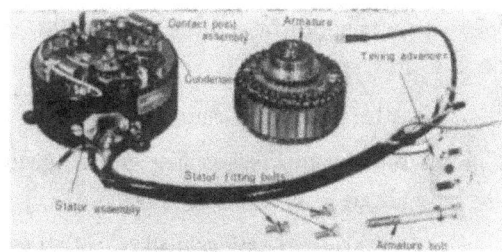

**Fig. 133**
STARTER DYNAMO ASSEMBLY

### (3) Operation

Refer to the wiring diagram when reading this section.

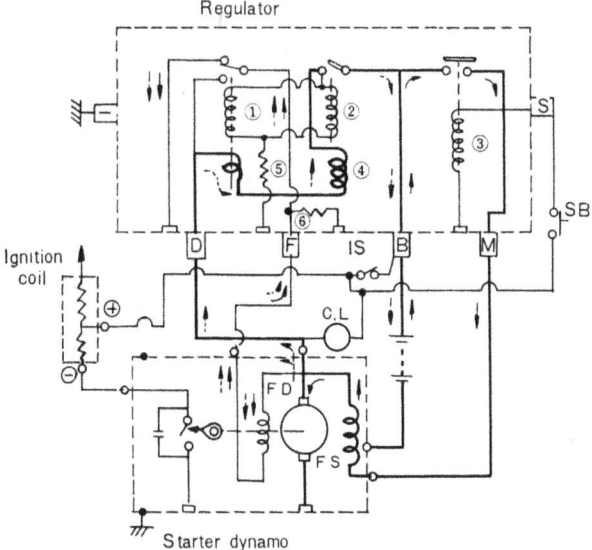

**Fig. 134**
WIRING DIAGRAM OF CHARGING AND STARTING SYSTEM

When the ignition switch (IS) is turned on and the starter button (SB) pushed, electric current flows from the battery to the switch relay coil (3) and the relay points contact.

When the starter switch relay points contact, a large electric current flows from the battery to the starter field coil (FS) and armature in the direction marked by the solid arrows in the diagram. The starter dynamo turns with a strong torque as an electric starter. An exciting current flows to the dynamo field coil (FD) and the regulator.

After the engine starts and the starter button is released, the starter switch relay coil points open. The dynamo field coil (FD) ceases to receive electric current from the battery and is supplied electric current from the armature, as shown by the dotted lines in the illustration.

The starter dynamo works as a dynamo and generates electricity to power electrical equipment and charge the battery.

When voltage generated in the dynamo rises because of an increase in the engine rpm, the cutout relay coil (2) is charged and the points contact. Battery charging commences.

If generated voltage becomes higher than the specified voltage, the operation of the voltage regulator coil (1) becomes strong. The voltage regulator points open and the field current is forced to pass through the regulating resistance (6). Field current decreases and the generated voltage is adjusted to a proper level.

If generated voltage continues to rise even though the voltage regulator points are open, the movable point contacts the lower contact point and short-circuits the dynamo field coil, dropping field current voltage to zero so that electricity cannot be generated.

Voltage is kept constant by these processes.

No damage occurs even if the starter button is pressed when the engine is running.

When the ignition switch is turned on before the engine is started, the B terminal, ignition switch, charge lamp and armature ground circuit is turned on and the charge indicator lamp lights.

When voltage increases and the cutout relay operates, the charge indicator lamp goes out.

If the charge indicator lamp does not turn off after the engine starts, it indicates that electricity is not being generated.

### (4) Inspection and Adjustments

Careful periodical inspection is recommended to prevent possible troubles in the starter dynamo.

(A) Inspection every 500 km (300 miles)

• Check the battery solution level and add pure distilled water up to the upper level line if necessary.

• Check to see that the regulator terminals are tight.

• Adjust contact breaker points gap to 0.3~0.4 mm (0.012~0.016 in).

(B) Inspection every 3,000km (1,900 miles)

• Perform the 500 km (300 miles) inspections.

• Check carbon brushes for wear and replace if worn to below 14 mm (0.55 in).

• Blow the commutator and carbon brushes clean with compressed air.

• Polish the contact point surfaces with fine emery paper and align them perfectly.

CAUTION: Oil or foreign particles dirtying the commutator can cause serious trouble. If the commutator has oil on it or carbon particles, etc., cannot be cleaned off with compressed air, remove the starter dynamo and wipe clean with a dry rag.

(C) Inspection every 5,000 km (3,000 miles), 7,000 km (4,500 miles) and 10,000 km (6,000 miles)

• Perform the 3,000 km (1,900 miles) inspections.

• Wipe the commutator with alcohol or benzine.

NOTE: After the motorcycle is ridden 10,000 km (6,000 miles), make inspections and adjustments listed above every 2,000~3,000 km (1,300~1,900 miles).

### (5) Dynamo Trouble Shooting

(A) If Starter Does Not Turn or Battery Is Not Charged Properly

• Check wiring harnesses for short circuits, breaks and loose connections.

• Check fuse and replace if burned out.

• Check battery. Check voltage and specific gravity of each cell. When all six cells are in same condition, charge the battery. If only one cell is discharged, the battery must be repaired or replaced.

• Check starter button and starter switch relay. Connect the battery positive (+) terminal to the regulator "M" terminal. If the starter turns, the trouble is in the starter switch or starter switch relay in the regulator.

• Check the dynamo. Check to see if the carbon brushes contact the commutator correctly. Check to see if the commutator is dirty with carbon particles. If there is no trouble with the brushes or commutator, check the field coils inside the stator.

(B) If Battery Is Not Charged

• Check wiring harnesses for short circuits, breaks and loose connections.

• Check voltage adjusting ability of the regulator by wiring as shown in Fig. 135.

△ Remove the regulator B terminal wiring going to the battery positive (+) terminal.

△ Connect a DC voltage meter.

△ Touch the wiring terminal removed from the B terminal with a red harness on which a fuse is installed to the M terminal and start the engine. Remove the terminal after the engine starts.

△ If the voltmeter reads between 14.5~15.5 volts at 2,000~4,000 engine rpm, the regulator and dynamo are not defective. If the meter reads less than 14.5 volts, the trouble is in the regulator or dynamo. To find which is defective, check the dynamo.

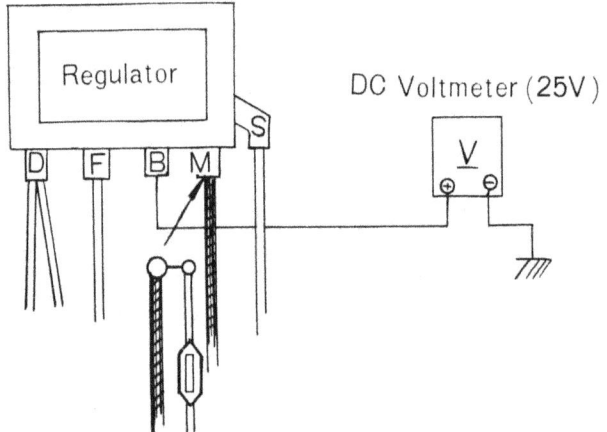

**Fig. 135**
CHECKING VOLTAGE ADJUSTING ABILITY

• Check the dynamo by keeping the engine rpm at 3,000 rpm and removing the wiring on the F terminal. Ground the wire for just an instant. If voltage rises to over 25 volts immediately, the dynamo is not defective and the trouble is in the regulator. If it does not, the trouble is in the dynamo.

CAUTION: Do not ground the wire for more than $\frac{1}{8} \sim \frac{1}{2}$ second at a time.

Before inspecting the dynamo, check to see if the carbon brushes seat properly and firmly and if the armature is in good condition.

# 2. Ignition System

A strong and "hot" spark with enough energy to ignite the compressed fuel/air mixture in the combustion chamber is necessary for gasoline engines. The ignition is timed precisely accoding to engine requirements.

The ignition coil produces high tension electric current. Proper ignition timing is controlled by an automatic timing advance system. The ignition coil is a kind of transformer which changes 12 volt battery current into high tension current of over 10,000 volts by using contact breakers and condensers.

## A. Operation

When the contact breaker points are closed electric current flows from the battery to the primary coil in the ignition coil. See Fig. 136.

When the cam turns with the turning of the crankshaft, the contact breaker points open and electric current to the primary coil is turned off.

Because of the abrupt fluctuation of this primary current, high tension current of 10,000 ~15,000 volts is induced in the secondary coil because of the vast difference in the number of windings in the two coils. The high tension current flows to the spark plug through the high tension cord. A spark jumps between the two electrodes in the spark plug and fuel in the combustion chamber is ignited.

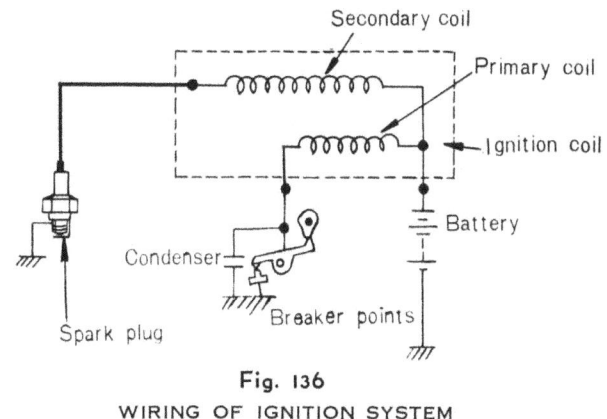

**Fig. 136**
WIRING OF IGNITION SYSTEM

## B. Construction of Ignition Coil

The primary coil and secondary coil are wound around an core made of silicon steel.

The primary coil is of comparatively thick enameled copper wire 0.15~1.0 mm (0.00197~0.0394 in) in diameter wound around the core 150~500 times. The secondary coil is of thin enameled wire 0.05~0.1 mm (0.000197~0.00394 in) in diameter wound around the core 13,000~20,000 times. The resistance of the primary coil is 3~5 $\Omega$ and that of the secondary coil is 6~15 $\Omega$.

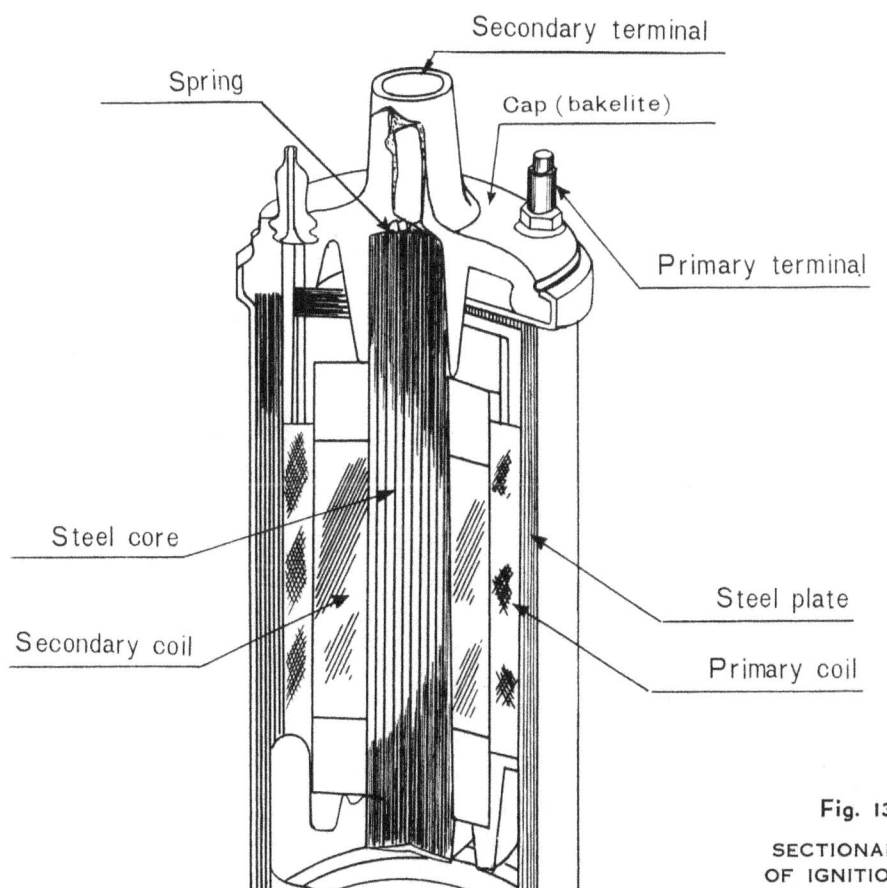

**Fig. 137**
SECTIONAL VIEW OF IGNITION COIL

(1) **Inspection**

Check the resistance of the primary and secondary coils first. If the resistance is correct, check the coils for spark performance with a three-prong gap tester. The coils are in good condition if a spark over 6 mm (0.24 in) in length is produced.

## C. Contact Breaker

The contact breaker connects and disconnects the primary circuit. It is a kind of switch and the following conditions must be met.

The contact breaker must connect and disconnect the primary circuit rapidly and firmly.

Electrical resistance including contact resistance must be small.

The contact breaker must operate precisely even at high rpm without jumping, etc.

Contact point surfaces must not be oxidized or deformed by high temperatures produced when 250~500 vots electric current is induced by the coil, sparks or Joule heat which is generated when the primary current is turned off.

Material which has small electrical resistance is usually soft and deforms easily. Tungsten steel is used for T10 contact breaker points.

Correct points gap is 0.3~0.4 mm (0.012~0.016 in).

## D. Condenser

It is necessary to disconnect the primary circuit as rapidly as possible to generate high tension current in the secondary coil. If a spark jumps between the contact breaker points, the current fluctuation is delayed and weakened and the voltage produced by the secondary coil is lowered. The condenser prevents sparking on the contact breaker points.

The condenser is connected to the contact breaker in parallel and absorbs electrical energy which would otherwise jump as sparks on the contact breaker points.

The condenser consists of two layers of tin foil with insulating paper seperating them, which are wound as shown in Fig. 138. The condenser is insulated with paraffin and sealed in a case.

When electricity enters the condenser, positive and negative current is charged into the two foils and electricity is discharged when both terminals are connected.

The capacity of the condenser indicates its ability to accumulate electricity and is measured in $\mu F$. If the capacity is too small, surplus energy cannot be absorbed by the condenser, causing a spark to jump in the contact breaker points. If the capacity of the condenser is too large, the secondary coil voltage is lowered and ignition at high rpm becomes poor.

The standard capacity of the condenser on the T10 is 0.22 $\mu F$ and the standard insulating resistance is over 5M$\Omega$. Replace it with a new one if its insulating resistance is below 1M$\Omega$.

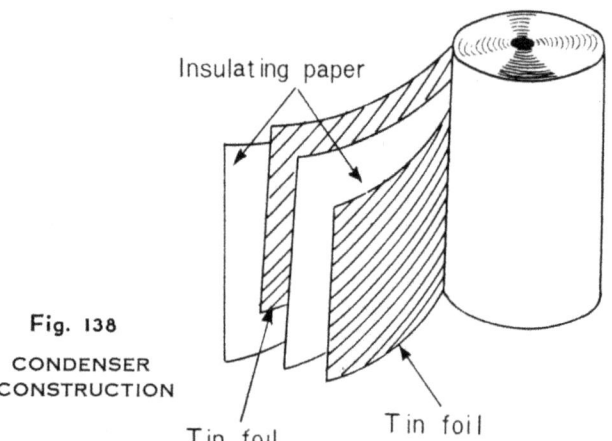

**Fig. 138** CONDENSER CONSTRUCTION

## E. Timing Advancer

When fuel in the combustion chamber is ignited by a spark from the spark plug, the fuel near the spark burns first and the fire spreads to fuel throughout the chamber, and pressure in the chamber reaches the maximum level. It takes a slight time for the fire to spread throughout the combustion chamber. Due to this combustion lag, the spark should be produced in the chamber before the piston reaches top dead center.

If ignition timing is set for normal engine speeds, pressure in the chamber reaches its maximum before the piston reaches top dead center when engine speed is low. This pressure sometimes stops the piston so that the engine runs backwards. Hard starting and rough running at low speeds will result.

On the contrary, if ignition timing is retarded for easier starting, the piston has already started its down stroke before pressure reaches the maximum at normal engine speeds, so that engine power is decreased and the engine overheats. Ignition timing must be changed according to engine speed.

A timing advancer is installed on the T10 for this purpose. The timing advancer plate is installed on the armature bolt, which is screwed into the crankshaft. Governor weights on this timing advancer plate are pulled in by timing advancer springs. As engine rpm increases, the weights move to the outside by centrifugal force and the cam is turned, advancing ignition timing. When engine rpm decreases, the strength of the timing advancer springs overcomes the centrifugal force and pulls the weights in, retarding ignition timing.

Ignition timing of the T10 is 7° before top dead center when timing is fully retarded and 30° before tdc when timing is fully advanced. Timing advance begins at 1,200 rpm and ends at 1,500 rpm.

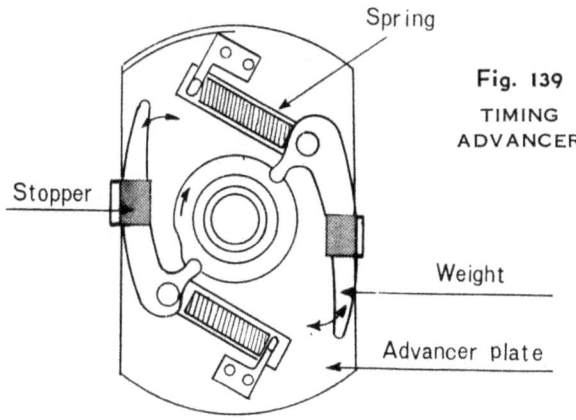

**Fig. 139 TIMING ADVANCER**

## F. Spark Plug

### (1) Construction

The spark plug is essential in a gasoline engine. It produces a spark in the combustion chamber when high tension electric current enters the center electrode and jumps to the side electrode. This spark ignites the compressed fuel/air mixture in the combustion chamber and the burning of this mixture creates gas pressure which pushes the piston down, turning the engine.

The spark plug is subjected to extremely high force of about 40 atmospheric pressures and high temperatures of over 2,000° C (3,600° F), as well as being buffeted by severe vibrations. It must be able to bear these adverse conditions and perform its function without interruption.

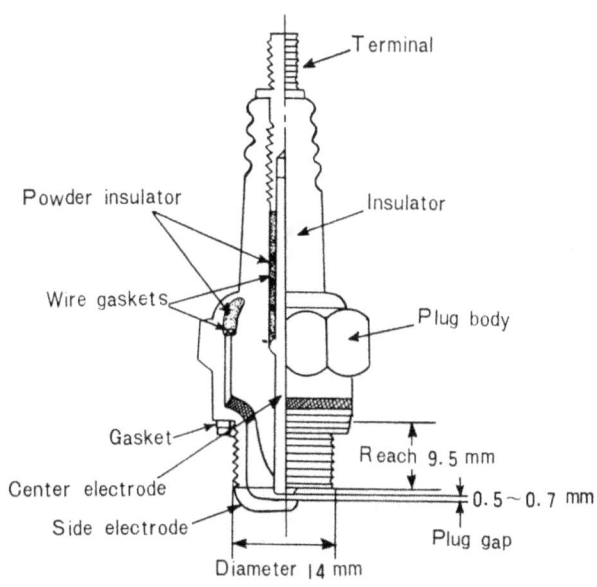

**Fig. 140 SECTIONAL VIEW OF SPARK PLUG**

### (2) Heat Range

The T10 uses 14 mm spark plugs with a reach of 9.5 mm. Not all spark plugs of this size are suitable, however, because different spark plugs have different heat dissipation characteristics, which is called heat range.

Different heat range spark plugs are needed for different engines because of variations in engine rpm, location of plugs, design of engine, heat produced, etc.

A spark plug with the improper heat range causes trouble in the engine. If the spark plug porcelain core overheats and its temperature becomes over 750° C (1,382° F), preignition will occur. If the porcelain core temperature is below 400° C (752° F), the plug cannot burn off oil and carbon deposits and the electrode is dirtied, so the engine misfires. Accordingly, a spark plug in which the porcelain core is kept between 400~750° C (752~1,382° F) must be used.

The standard spark plug for the T10 is NGK B-7. If the standard plug is not available, choose a correct spark plug by referring to the Spark Plug Conversion Chart. If the motorcycle is ridden only at slow speeds, use a NGK B-6 spark plug.

## (3) Conversion Chart

| NGK | Champion | AC | Autolit | Bosch | KLG |
|---|---|---|---|---|---|
| B-6 | J-7 | 45, 45-Com | A-5 | W175T3 | TFS50 |
|     | J-6 | 44, 44-Com |     |        |       |
| B-7 | J-5 | 43, 43-Com | AT-4 | W225T3 | FS70 |
|     |     | 42, 42-Com | A-3  |        | FS75 |

# 3. Safety Devices

## A. Turn Signal Relay

The turn signal relay on the T10 is a condenser type which is little affected by vibrations, unlike some types of relays.

When the ignition switch (S) is turned on, an electric current from the battery flows in the relay B terminal, contact point P and coil L1 circuit, causing the contact point to vibrate from the charging of coil L1. When the condenser becomes fully charged, the flow of the electric current ceases and the vibration of the contact point stops. Therefore, when the ignition switch is turned on the condenser is always in a charged condition.

When the turn signal switch (WS) is turned on with the condenser fully charged, electricity charged into the turn signal relay condenser discharges through coil L1, coil L2 and lamps WL. The magnetic power of coils L1 and L2 makes the points open. Discharging current from the condenser is so small, however, that the lamps are not lighted.

When the discharging of the condenser is completed, the contact points close, turning on the turn signal lamps. Electric current flows in coil L1 and coil L2, but the magnetic power in the two coils cancels out each other so that the magnetic power does not affect the contact points. The contact points remain closed and the turn signal lamps remain lighted until the condenser is charged again and the magnetic power of coil L1 is lost. Then the contact points open as the movable point is pulled by the magnetic power of coil L2 and the turn signal lamps are turned off. The condenser begins charging again.

These operations are repeated automatically, and the turn signal lamps flash off and on 75~95 times per minute.

If the turn signal relay is not grounded perfectly, the condenser will not be charged properly, the relay does not operate and the contact points are burned. Install the turn signal relay on the frame carefully.

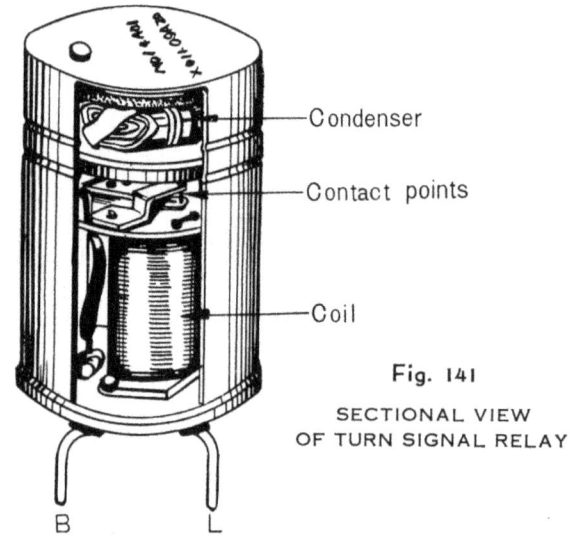

Fig. 141
SECTIONAL VIEW OF TURN SIGNAL RELAY

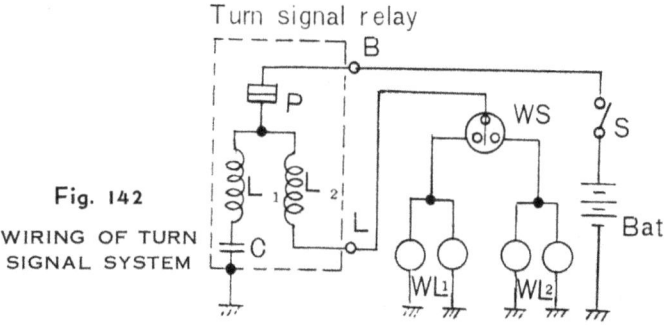

Fig. 142
WIRING OF TURN SIGNAL SYSTEM

## B. Horn

### (1) Construction

The construction of the horn is shown in Fig. 143.

When electric current flows in the coil the

iron core is magnetized, which pulls the moving plate. The moving plate vibrates the diaphragm, which makes a sound. The trumpet resonates this sound and controls volume and tone.

Contact points connect and disconnect the electrical circuit to the coil. An anti-arc resistor or condenser prevents a spark from jumping between the contact point surfaces and burning them.

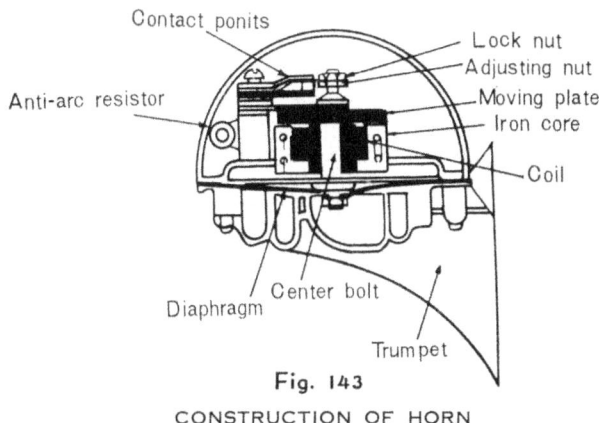

Fig. 143
CONSTRUCTION OF HORN

(2) Operation

When the horn button is pushed, electric current flows to the coil and the iron core is magnetized. The moving plate is pulled, but when the moving plate is moved the contact points are opened immediately and the magnetic power of the iron core is lost. The moving plate returns to its normal position. This operation is repeated very rapidly and continuously.

The diaphragm, which is connected to the moving plate with a center bolt, vibrates and makes a small sound. The trumpet resonates the sound and increases its volume.

The coil induces high tension electric current which could burn the contact points, so an anti-arc resistor or condenser is installed to absorb this current. Both an anti-arc resistor and a condenser are used on T10 motorcycles.

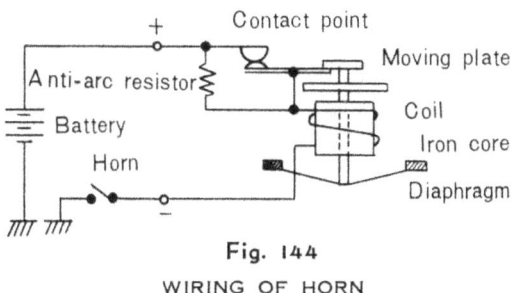

Fig. 144
WIRING OF HORN

## C. Battery

The battery consists of positive and negative plates immersed in electrolyte solution. It can be charged and store electricity and supply a considerable amount of electric current without the voltage varying. A Yuasa 12 volt 12 ampere hour battery is installed in the T10.

During daytime use, the battery supplies electric current to the ignition system, horn, turn signal lamps, neutral indicator lamp, charge indicator lamp and brake lamp. For night riding, in additon to these the battery supplies current for the head lamp and tail lamp.

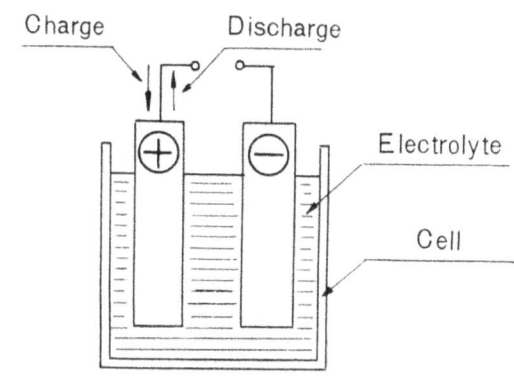

Fig. 145
SECTIONAL VIEW OF BATTERY

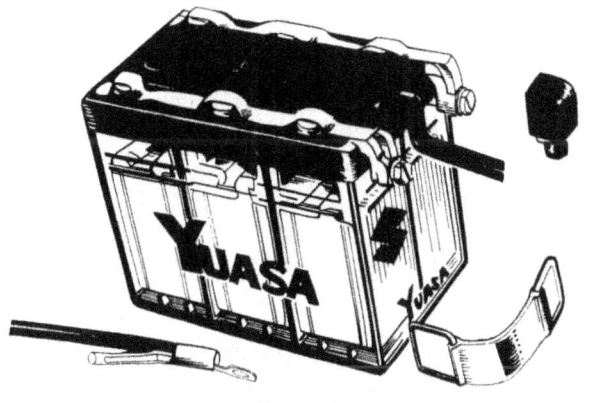

Fig. 146
BATTERY

(1) Specifications

| | |
|---|---|
| Type | Yuasa MBK 7-12A |
| Voltage | 12 |
| Capacity | 12 AH/10 hours |
| Dimensions (L×W×H) | 170×101×143 mm (6.7×4×5.6 in) |
| Weight including electrolyte | 5.5 kg (12 lb) |
| Quantity of electrolyte | 1.0 liter (2.1 pt) |

## (2) Construction

Positive and negative plates are installed in the cells alternately, with insulators separating them. The cell is filled with electrolyte solution. One cell supplies about 2.1 volts of electricity. The T10 battery consists of six cells connected in series to supply 12 volt electric current.

(A) Positive Plates

The positive plate consists of a frame of lead antimony alloy filled with kneaded lead powder or lead oxide.

As the positive electrode is fragile, excessive shocks or vibration, abrupt charging and discharging and too high specific gravity of the electrolyte solution can damage it, lowering battery capacity. Handle the battery carefully.

(B) Negative Plates

The negative plate is the same size as the positive plate. It is made of spongy lead. The negative plate can be damaged or shrunk in size by excessive shocks or vibration or abrupt charging and discharging.

CAUTION: If the battery is discharged excessively, unreducible white sulphuric lead is produced and it is impossible to charge the battery. If foreign particles such as iron, etc., get into the battery solution, discharging is hastened even if the battery is not used.

Special care should be taken when checking the battery solution specific gravity or adding to the solution.

(C) Insulators

Plastic insulators are used to prevent short circuits between the positive and negative plates.

(D) Fiberglass Mats

Fiberglass/felt mats are fitted on both sides of the positive plates and compressed with $0.1 \sim 0.2$ kg-cm$^2$ ($1.4 \sim 2.8$ lb-in) of pressure to prevent damage to the positive plates. The diameter of the fiberglass threads in the mat is $5 \sim 30$ microns in diameter.

(E) Cells

Resistance to harmful effects of heat, cold, shock and corrosion is necessary for cell materials. The T10 has a cell made of plastic, which is proof against these conditions, easily manufactured and clear so that the level of the battery solution can be observed easily.

(F) Electrolyte

Diluted sulphuric acid with a specific gravity of 1.280 is used in the battery. As the specific gravity of the solution changes according to the amount of charge in the battery, battery capacity can be checked by measuring the specific gravity of the solution. Excessively high or low specific gravity shortens the life of the battery and causes troubles such as rapid discharge without use and insufficient battery capacity. Always check the battery solution specific gravity as well as the level of the solution.

## (3) Operation

Chemical changes in the battery are shown in the illustration. When the battery is fully charged, the positive plate is lead peroxide and the negative plate is spongy lead. As discharging progresses, sulphuric lead is produced by both plates and the solution becomes water. When the plates change into sulphuric lead, electricity is generated. When electricity is supplied to the battery from an outside source, the sulphuric lead is changed into lead peroxide and spongy lead.

Sulphuric lead produced by normal use is reducible and the battery can be used again when it is properly charged. If the battery is used until it holds very little electricity, however, the sulphuric lead becomes unreducible. This condition is called sulphation.

CAUTION: Do not use a battery after it has been discharged by 50 per cent. If the battery capacity falls below 50 per cent, recharge it.

| Specific gravity | Positive Plate | Electrolyte Solution | Negative Plate |
|---|---|---|---|
| high ↑ ↓ low | lead peroxide $PbO_2$  ———  sulphuric lead $PbSO_4$ | dilute sulphuric acid $2H_2SO_4$ ↑ charging  water $2H_2O$ | spongy lead $Pb$  ———  sulphuric lead $PbSO_4$ |

discharging ↓

Fig. 147
BATTERY OPERATION

## (4) Capacity

The battery capacity indicates the amount of electricity the battery can supply before it is discharged. Ampere hour (AH) is usually used to measure the capacity, that is AH = discharge current (A) × discharge hours (H).

Battery capacity changes, however, according to the rate of discharge. When the rate increases battery capacity is lowered because the chemical changes in the battery cannot be made rapidly. To show battery capacity more accurately, therefore, it is measured in AH/Hr. If a fully charged battery takes "T" hours to discharge at a rate of 1 amphere the battery has a capacity of 1 TAH/"T" Hr. The capacity of the T10 battery is 12 AH/10 Hr, that is, it takes ten hours to discharge at a rate of 1.2 ampere.

Check the amount of charge in the battery by measuring the specific gravity of the battery solution at 20° C (68° F) and referring to the table below.

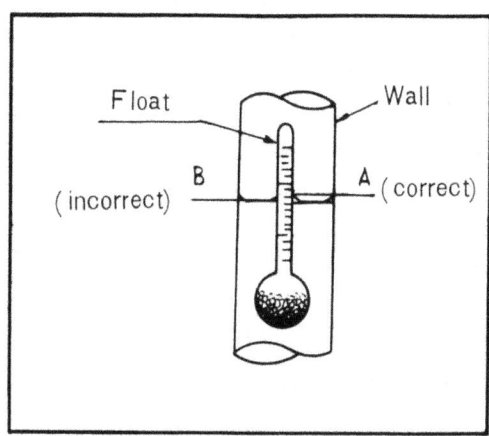

Fig. 148
READING HYDROMETER

Battery solution specific gravity changes according to its temperature. When the specific gravity is checked, convert the reading to the 20° C (68° F) standard with the following formula:

$S_{20} = S_t - 0.0007(t - 20)$

$S_{20}$ is specific gravity at 20° C (68° F)
$S_t$ is reading of hydrometer
$t$ is temperature of solution

Relation between Specific Gravity and Temperature

| Specific Gravity | Battery Capacity |
|---|---|
| 1.280 | 100% |
| 1.250 | 75% |
| 1.220 | 50% |
| 1.190 | 25% |
| 1.160 | almost discharged |
| 1.130 | fully discharged |

Check the specific gravity carefully.

Do not let the hydrometer float touch the wall of the vessel.

Read the hydrometer scale at "A", not at "B". See the illustration.

| Temperature | −10°C (14°F) | 0°C (32°F) | 10°C (50°F) | 20°C (68°F) | 30°C (86°F) | 40°C (104°F) |
|---|---|---|---|---|---|---|
| Specific Gravity | 1.321 | 1.314 | 1.307 | 1.300 | 1.293 | 1.286 |
| | 1.311 | 1.304 | 1.297 | 1.290 | 1.283 | 1.276 |
| | 1.301 | 1.294 | 1.287 | 1.280 | 1.273 | 1.266 |
| | 1.291 | 1.284 | 1.277 | 1.270 | 1.263 | 1.256 |
| | 1.281 | 1.274 | 1.267 | 1.260 | 1.253 | 1.246 |
| | 1.271 | 1.264 | 1.257 | 1.250 | 1.243 | 1.236 |
| | 1.261 | 1.254 | 1.247 | 1.240 | 1.233 | 1.226 |
| | 1.251 | 1.244 | 1.237 | 1.230 | 1.223 | 1.216 |
| | 1.241 | 1.234 | 1.227 | 1.220 | 1.213 | 1.206 |
| | 1.231 | 1.224 | 1.217 | 1.210 | 1.203 | 1.196 |
| | 1.221 | 1.214 | 1.207 | 1.200 | 1.193 | 1.186 |
| | 1.211 | 1.204 | 1.197 | 1.190 | 1.183 | 1.176 |
| | 1.201 | 1.194 | 1.187 | 1.180 | 1.173 | 1.166 |

### (5) Capacity and Solution Temperature

Chemical change in the battery is active at high temperatures and the battery delivers good performance. When the temperature lowers, however, the battery activity decreases. At 15° C below zero (5° F), the battery capacity is about 50 per cent of the capacity at 20° C (68° F).

When only low current is drawn from the battery this creates no problem, but when the battery is used for the electric starter, which requires large current, its performance can be affected.

In cold climates the battery is more liable to become fully discharged. Special care of the battery is required and frequent checks of the specific gravity, and possible charging, is necessary.

### (6) Adding to Solution

When the percentage of sulphuric acid in the solution is high, chemical changes in the battery are active and good performance results. If, however, the positive plate and insulator are corroded by a solution containing too much sulphuric acid serious trouble is caused by damage to the plate. When the plate is damaged, battery capacity drops suddenly and the battery may be short circuited. Life of the battery is shortened.

CAUTION: Do not add sulphuric acid to the battery solution. Add only pure distilled water to bring the solution level up to the upper line.

### (7) Auto-Discharge

The battery discharges slowly when it is not used for a long time. Spongy lead of the negative plate combines chemically with the sulphuric acid naturally, producing sulphuric lead and discharging the battery. When the temperature is high, the battery discharges more rapidly because of the increased pace of chemical changes in the battery.

At normal temperatures, the battery discharges about 1 per cent of battery capacity daily. If the battery is not charged before it becomes fully discharged, it may not be able to take a charge again.

CAUTION: Charge the battery once a month when not in use.

Foreign particles such as iron, copper, salt, etc., in the solution hastens the discharge of the battery and can cause sulfation. Do not add anything other than pure distilled water to the battery solution.

### (8) Initial Charging

The battery can be stored for a long period of time when it is sealed and does not contain battery solution, so batteries are normally stocked in this condition. An initial charge is required before the battery can be used.

The battery must be charged at a slow rate for many hours for the initial charge.

A dry charged battery is installed in the T10. It requires 15~20 hours of initial charging. If the battery is not charged completely at the time of initial charging, it will never be able to take a full charge and cannot deliver good performance. The life of the battery will be shortened as well.

(A) How to Charge

Remove the battery from the vinyl bag. Remove sealing tape from the filler hole plugs. Do not remove the sealing tape until ready to give the battery its initial charge.

The end of the vent tube is sealed, so cut off about 15 mm ($\frac{1}{2}$ in) of it. If the end of the tube is not cut off or if the tube is pinched shut between the frame and the battery or clogged, gas generated during operation cannot be exhausted and sometimes the battery case will crack.

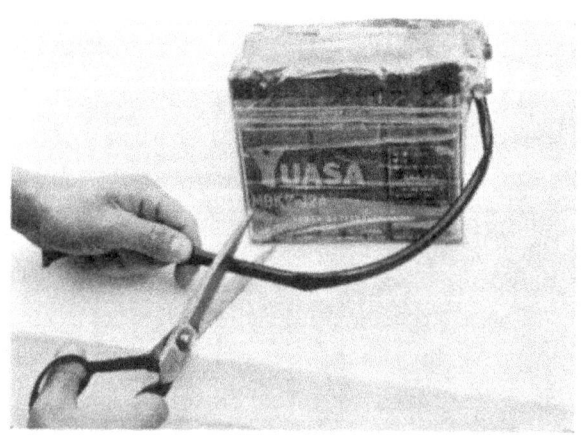

**Fig. 149**
CUTTING AIR VENT TUBE

Connect the battery positive terminal to the positive terminal of the battery charger and the negative terminal to the negative terminal of the charger. When charging two or more batteries simultaneously, connect them as shown in Fig. 150.

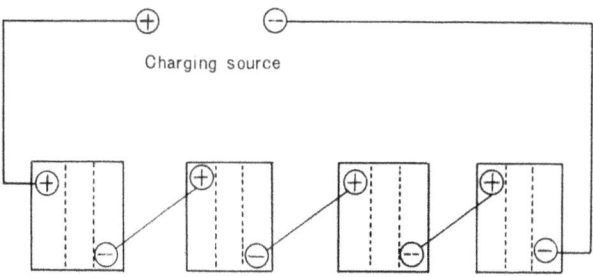

Fig. 150
CONNECTIONS WHEN CHARGING BATTERIES

Remove the filler plugs. Pour diluted sulphuric acid with a specific gravity of 1.280 at 20° C (68° F) into the filler holes until it reaches the upper level line. Cool the electrolyte to 20° C (68° F) before pouring it into the battery.

Let the battery stand for 2~3 hours before charging. If the solution level falls below the lower level line, add electrolyte up to the upper level line.

Charge the battery for 15~20 hours with 1.2 ampere electric current.

If the temperature of the solution rises to more than 45° C (113° F), stop the charging or decrease the charging current by one-half.

Do not use larger than 1.2 ampere current to charge the battery, or the life of the battery will be shortened.

If the battery is not used for over 6 months after manufacture, it should be charged for 60 hours. The date of manufacture is given on top of the battery.

If the solution level lowers during charging, add pure distilled water up to the upper level line.

Two or three hours before the charging is completed, adjust the specific gravity of the solution to 1.280 at 20° C (68° F).

Explosive gas is produced during charging, so do not use a fire near the battery.

After initial charging is finished, adjust the solution level to the upper limit line, insert the filler plugs and tighten them with a screw driver.

Wash the battery clean of sulphuric acid with fresh water.

Put the battery in the vinyl cover and install on the motorcycle, making sure that the vent tube is not pinched shut. Insert it through the hole immediately in front of the rear swinging arm pivot shaft just behind the engine.

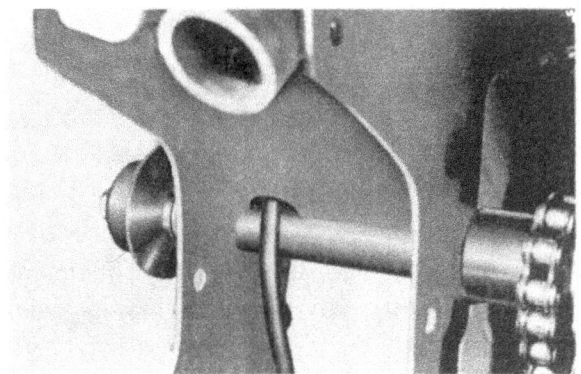

Fig. 151
INSERTING BATTERY AIR VENT TUBE

# PERIODICAL SERVICING

## 1. Adjusting Ignition Timing

As ignition timing tends to get out of adjustment gradually, check the timing every 3,000km (1,900 miles) and readjust as necessary.

### A. Left Cylinder

Rotate the crankshaft counterclockwise as seen from the dynamo side with a wrench until the left cylinder contact points gap (c) is at its widest point and stop the crankshaft there.

Loosen screw (d) and adjust the left cylinder points gap (c) to 0.3~0.4 mm (0.012~0.016 in) by turning point gap adjuster eccentric screw (g).

Tighten screw (d) firmly.

Loosen two screws (e) and move the contact point base until the points begin to open just as stator notch (a) is in line with timing advancer red notch (b), which is the red notch without a "+" mark.

Tighten screws (e) firmly.

This adjustment must be made when the timing advancer is not in an advanced position. If the cam is fully advanced, the points should begin to open when stator notch (a) is in line with timing advancer red notch (b') with a "+" mark.

### B. Right Cylinder

Rotate the crankshaft 180°.

Loosen screw (d') and adjust the right cylinder contact points gap (c') to 0.3~0.4 mm (0.012~0.016 in) by turning point gap adjuster eccentric screw (g'). Tighten screw (d') firmly.

Loosen two screws (e') and adjust contact point base until the points begin to open just as stator notch (a) is in line with timing advancer blue notch (f), which is the blue notch without the "+" mark.

This adjustment must be made when the timing advancer is not in an advanced position. If the cam is fully advanced, the points should begin to open when stator notch (a) is in line with timing advancer blue notch (f') which has a "+" mark.

Tighten screws (e') firmly.

Moving contact point base clockwise advances ignition timing.

Moving contact point base counterclockwise retards ignition timing.

Standard ignition timing is 7° before top dead center (no advance) to 30° before top dead center (fully advanced).

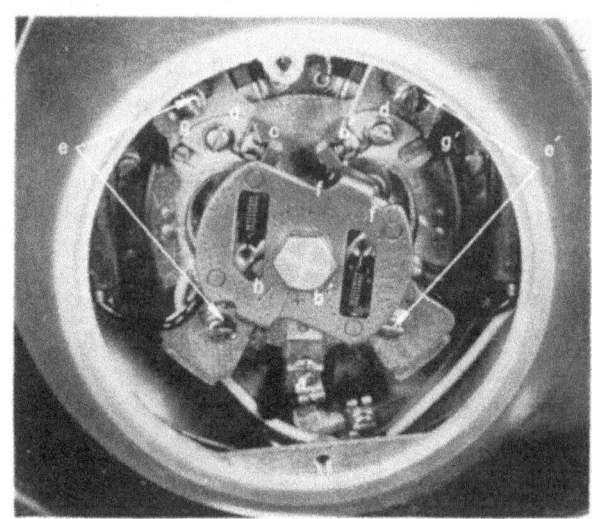

**Fig. 152**
IGNITION TIMING

### C. Adjusting Timing with Gauge

Ignition timing can be adjusted more accurately by measuring the position of the piston with a gauge.

• Adjust contact points gap as outlined in previous section.

• Remove the cylinder head.

• Rotate the crankshaft forward, i.e. counterclockwise when seen from the dynamo side, until the points are just prior to opening.

To find this point accurately:

Turn the ignition switch on, rotate the crankshaft forward gently until just before a spark jumps in the spark plug; or,

Turn the ignition switch on, wire a lamp or buzzer between the contact breaker point arm and the engine and rotate the crankshaft forward gently until just before the lamp turns on or the sound of buzzer changes.

Touch the feeler of the timing gauge to the piston, adjust the dial to zero, rotate the crankshaft forward and measure the distance the piston travels to reach top dead center.

The piston should be 0.27 mm (0.0166 in) below top dead center at 7° ignition timing (no advance) and 4.76 mm (0.188 in) below top dead center at 30° ignition timing (fully advanced).

If the piston is in a position different from this, adjust ignition timing as described in the previous section.

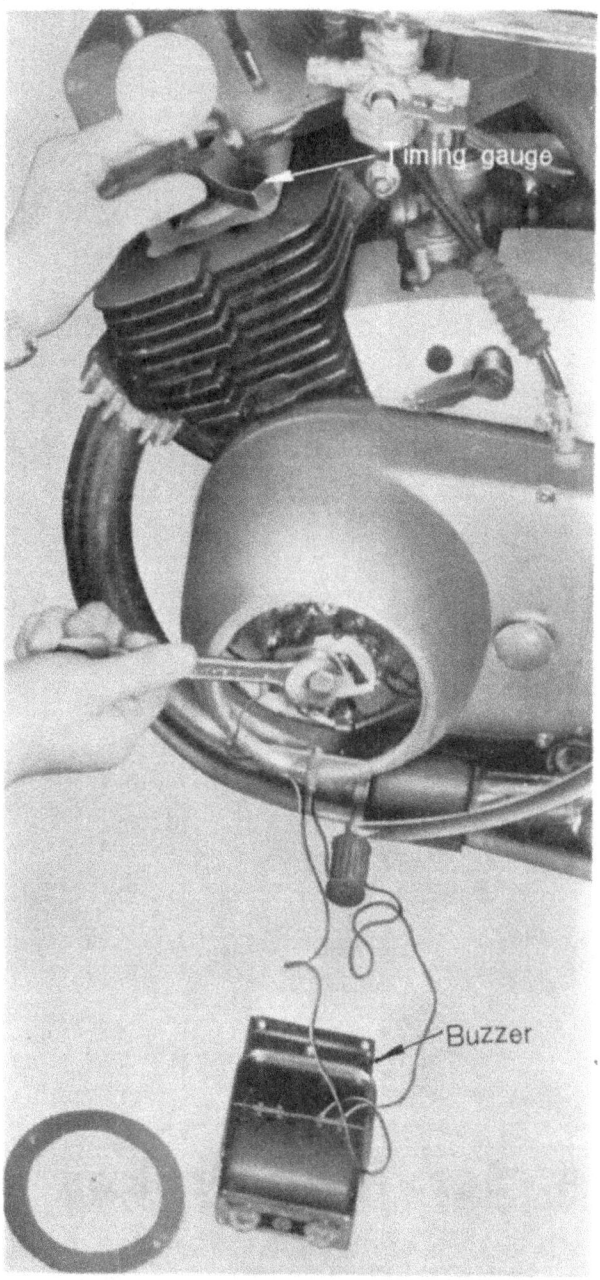

**Fig. 153**
ADJUSTING TIMING WITH GAUGE

(1) **Timing Gauge**

Suzuki Motor stocks this timing gauge, which will be supplied upon order.

| Dial Gauge | |
|---|---|
| Measuring range | 10mm (0.39 in) |
| Measuring unit | 0.01mm (0.00039 in) |

| Dial Gauge Holder | |
|---|---|
| Small, | for all Suzuki 50 cc and 80 cc models, SG and SK 125 cc models and SGB and SKB 150 cc models. |
| Large, | for all Suzuki 250 cc models and SH 125 cc model |

| Container | wooden box |
|---|---|

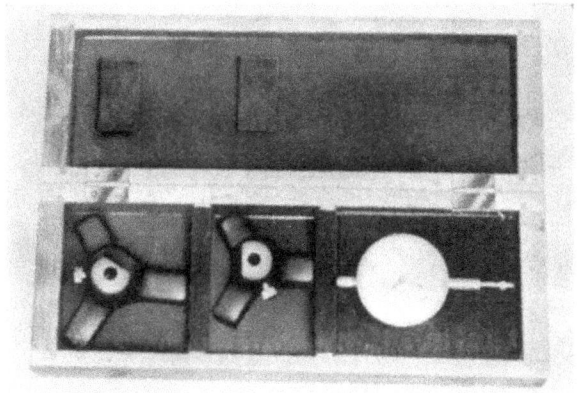

**Fig. 154**
TIMING GAUGE

# 2. Cleaning Spark Plugs & Adjusting Gap

The standard spark plug gap is 0.5~0.7mm (0.02~0.028 in). Adjust spark plug gap every 3,000 km (1,900 miles).

The standard spark plug is NGK B-7.

Remove carbon deposits from the spark plug with a spark plug cleaner or wire every 3,000 km (1,900 miles).

Use of the standard NGK B-7 spark plug is highly recommended for good performance.

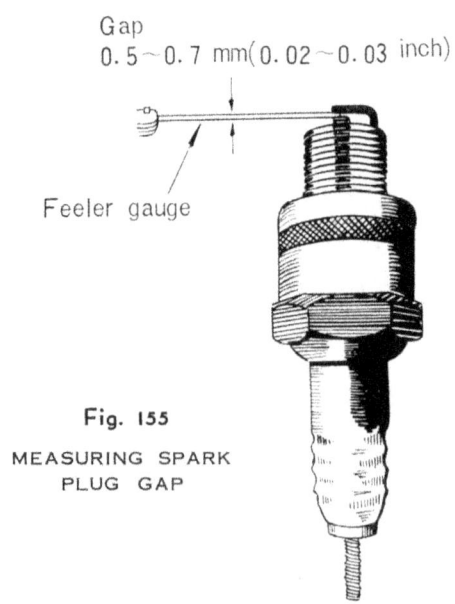

Fig. 155
MEASURING SPARK PLUG GAP

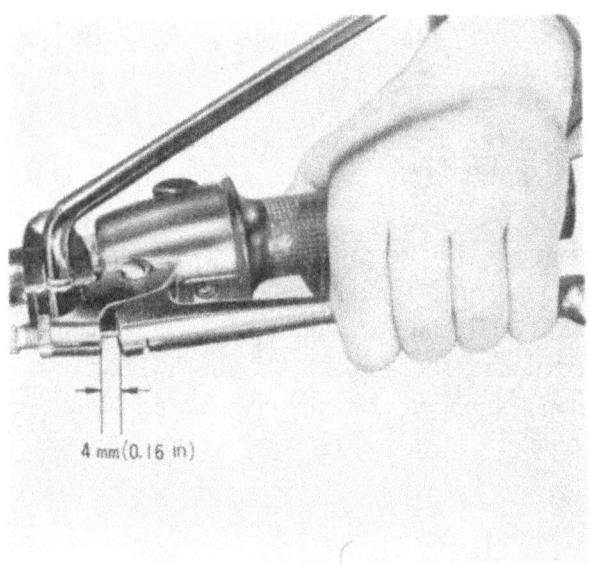

Fig. 157
FREE PLAY OF CLUTCH LEVER

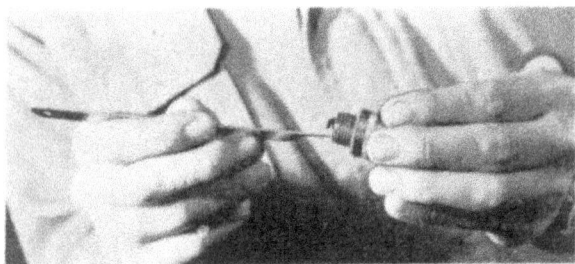

Fig. 156
CLEANING SPARK PLUG

## 3. Adjusting Clutch

Check the clutch every 3,000 km (1,900 miles) and adjust if necessary.

Proper free play of the clutch lever is 4mm (0.16 in) measured at the clutch lever base.

Clutch lever free play can be adjusted with the clutch cable adjuster located on the crankcase right cover.

Screwing adjuster out decreases play.

Screwing adjuster in increases play.

If adjustment cannot be made with the clutch cable adjuster, adjust with the clutch adjusting screw located on the side of the crankcase left cover.

Screwing in clutch adjusting screw makes the clutch easier to disengage.

Screwing out clutch adjusting screw makes the clutch harder to disengage.

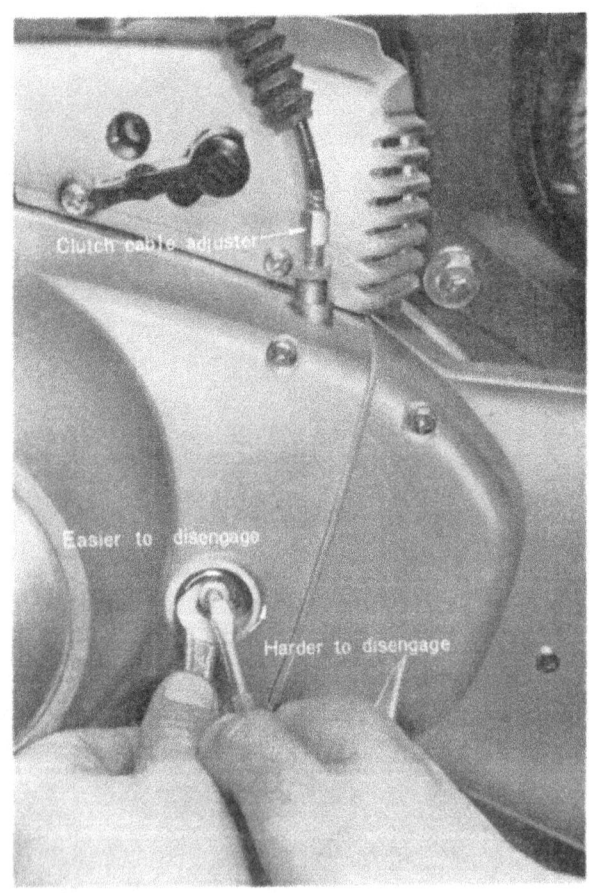

Fig. 158
ADJUSTING CLUTCH WITH ADJUSTING SCREW

## 4. Servicing Brakes

Check and service brakes every 3,000 km (1,900 miles).

## A. Adjusting Front Brake

The front brake should be fully applied when the front brake lever is 20 mm (0.8 in) from the throttle grip.

Turning front brake adjuster in decreases play.

Turning front brake adjuster out increases play.

Turning rear brake adjuster in decreases travel.

Turning rear brake adjuster out increases travel. Adjust the brake pedal play to 2~3 mm (0.08~0.12). Remove air from the system.

Check the amount of oil in the brake oil tank every 3,000 km (1,900 miles) and add if necessary.

Change brake oil every 10,000 km (6,000 miles). See the hydraulic brake section on page 55.

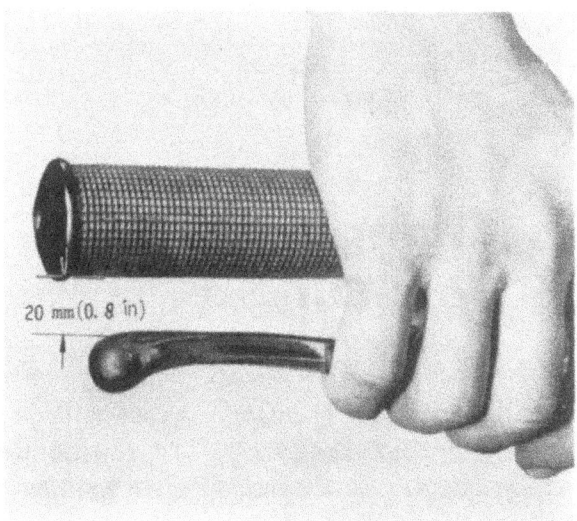

**Fig. 159**
BRAKE LEVER PLAY

**Fig. 161**
BRAKE PEDAL TRAVEL

**Fig. 160**
ADJUSTING FRONT BRAKE

**Fig. 162**
ADJUSTING REAR BRAKE

## B. Adjusting Rear Brake

The brake pedal should have a travel of 25~30 mm (1~1.2 in).

Travel is controlled by the rear brake adjuster.

# 5. Adjusting Head Lamp Beam

The height of the head lamp beam can be adjusted by loosening the bolts on both sides of the head lamp housing and moving the unit up or down.

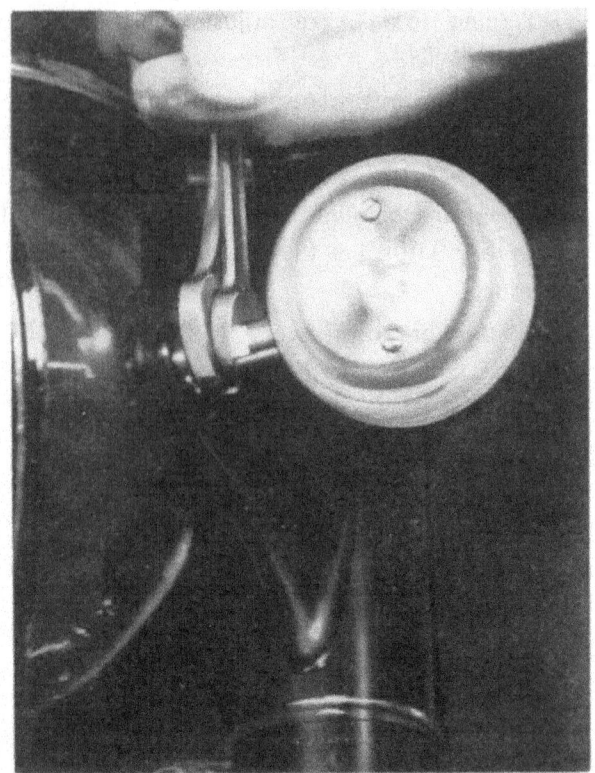

Fig. 163
ADJUSTING HEAD LAMP BEAM

## 6. Tire Pressure

|  | Front Tire | Rear Tire |
|---|---|---|
| Solo Riding | 1.1~1.3 kg/cm² (16~18 psi) | 1.8~2.0 kg/cm² (26~28 psi) |
| Dual Riding | 1.1~1.3 kg/cm² (16~18 psi) | 2.3~2.4 kg/cm² (32~34 psi) |

## 7. Adjusting Engine Idling

See "Adjusting Idling" in carburetor section.

## 8. Cleaning Air Cleaners

Remove the carburetor covers and air cleaner tube clamps. Remove the air cleaners and air cleaner tubes from the motorcycle together.
Clean the air cleaners by blowing compressed air from the inside every 3,000 km (1,900 miles) as shown in Fig. 164.
Replace them with new ones every 10,000km) 6,000 miles).

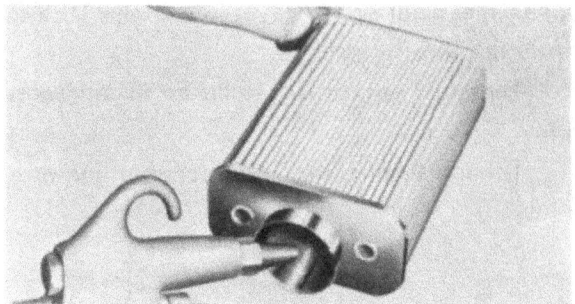

Fig. 164
CLEANING AIR CLEANER

## 9. Changing Gear Box Oil

As oil loses its lubricating efficiency when used too long, it is necessary to change the oil in the gear box periodically. To change the oil, remove the oil drain plug on the bottom of the engine and the oil filler plug on the upper part of the engine and drain out all of the used oil. Replace the oil drain plug. Remove the oil level screw. Pour in fresh oil through the oil filler hole until it begins to overflow through the oil level screw hole. About 500 cc (1.05 US pts) of oil is required. Be sure to replace the oil filler plug and oil level screw and tighten both securely. Use a good brand of SAE# 30~40 motor oil.

Change the oil after the first 500 km (300 miles) and every 3,000 km (1,900 miles) thereafter.

In the regions where the temperature falls below 10°C (50° F) in the morning, however, the use of 20W/40 multigrade motor oil is recommended.

Fig. 165
OIL DRAIN PLUG

# 10. Cleaning Muffler Baffle Pipes

Remove baffle pipe fitting screw. Pull the baffle pipe out of the muffler toward the rear of the motorcycle.

If the baffle pipe is not very dirty, wash with gasoline or cleaning solvent.

If the baffle pipe is very dirty with hard-caked carbon deposits, heat with a burner to burn off carbon deposits. After it cools, strike it gently to shake off the cinders.

The baffle pipe can also be cleaned by boiling in caustic soda solution for four or five hours and then washing with fresh water.

Fig. 167
PULLING BAFFLE PIPE OUT

Fg. 166

# 11. Cleaning Exhaust Pipes

Remove exhaust pipe from the engine. The exhaust pipe can be removed faster by removing the two muffler fitting bolts first. This step is not essential, but it is faster.

Remove carbon from inside the pipe by scraping with a screw driver or pulling a length of old drive chain back and forth through it.

Check exhaust pipe for dents. A seriously dented pipe is apt to accumulate carbon and adversely affect engine performance, and should be replaced with a new exhaust pipe.

Check the exhaust pipe gasket and replace with a new one if damaged or worn. Always replace any exhaust pipe gasket which leaks.

Be sure to fit the gasket properly when installing the exhaust pipe. Tighten fitting nuts evenly with a torque of 100 kg-cm (85 lb-in).

# 12. Drive Chain and Sprocket Maintenance

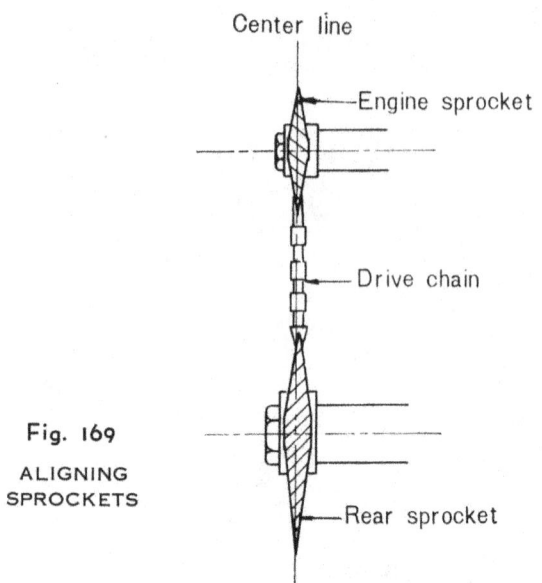

Fig. 169
ALIGNING SPROCKETS

## A. Inspecting Sprockets

If the engine sprocket or rear sprocket is excessively worn, drive chain slips, noise is produced, chain wear is hastened or chain is apt to jump off of sprocket. Even a new chain will not fit properly. Replace worn sprocket with a new one.

To inspect sprocket for wear fit a new drive chain and check to see if there is play between the chain links and sprocket teeth.

Inspect sprockets every 6,000 km (3,700 miles).

Fig. 168
CHECKING ENGINE SPROCKET WEAR

## B. Installing Sprockets

If the engine sprocket and rear sprocket are not aligned correctly, the drive chain is apt to jump off of the sprocket and drive chain wear and sprocket wear is hastened. Align the center of the two sprockets as shown in Fig. 169.

## C. Drive Chain

If the drive chain is slack it is apt to jump off of the sprocket and produces noise as well as wearing rapidly. If the drive chain is too tight, chain and sprocket wear is hastened and in some instances the chain will break under a sudden load.

The drive chain slackens gradually as the motorcycle is used from wearing of chain pins or links. When the chain becomes slack, adjust with drive chain adjusters.

### (1) Adjusting

Inspect and service the drive chain every 3,000 km (1,900 miles).

1. Remove chain inspection hole cap.
2. Loosen rear axle nut.
3. Use chain adjusters to adjust free play at center of drive chain to 30~40 mm (1.2~1.6 in) with the motorcycle on the center stand.

The play should be 10~15 mm (0.4~0.6 in) when the motorcycle is standing on the wheels.

A little more play is needed when carrying a passenger or a heavy load.

Turning chain adjusters in decreases play.

Turning chain adjusters out increases play.

CAUTION: Be sure to turn both adjusters the same amount, or wheels will not be kept in alignment.

**Fig. 170**
ADJUSTING DRIVE CHAIN

chain disconnect.

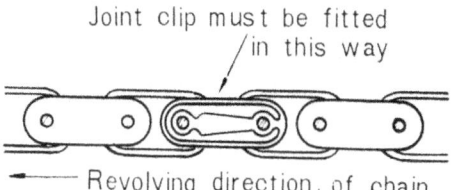

**Fig. 171**
CHAIN JOINT CLIP INSTALLATION

4. Tighten rear axle nut and check play in drive chain again.

Play will be decreased about 5mm (0.2 in) when the axle nut is tightened, so make allowances for this.

5. After drive chain play is adjusted, turn rear wheel and lubricate chain completely with spindle oil.

If the drive chain cannot be adjusted with the chain adjusters and is still slack, remove two links from the chain. If the chain still cannot be adjusted, replace with a new drive chain. If more than two chain links are removed, the pitch of the drive chain will not fit the sprocket teeth. Do not remove more than two links.

The T10 drive chain has 94 links including one joint link, a 15.875 mm (0.625 in) pitch, 10.16 mm (0.4 in) roller diameter, 5.08 mm (0.2 in) pin diameter and 18.4 mm (0.72 in) pin length.

### (2) Maintenance

Every 6,000 km (3,700 miles), remove the drive chain and inspect it carefully for seized links, wear, etc. Replace if badly worn or if there is much side play.

Wash the chain in cleaning solvent, drain and dry. Soak the chain in melted grease for several minutes or soak overnight in light engine oil. Drain and dry. Install on the motorcycle.

### (3) Tips on Installing Chain Joint Clip

Fit the chain joint clip with the trailing, or open end to the rear as the chain moves. as shown in Fig. 171. If the joint clip is installed with the open end facing the direction of chain movement, it may come off while riding and the

# 13. Adjusting Brake Lamp Switch

Be sure the brake lamp works properly, as it is an important safety device which warns following traffic that the motorcycle is being slowed.

The brake lamp switch can be adjusted by raising or lowering the switch assembly. There should be about 5 mm (0.2 in) of play after the brake pedal is depressed before the brake lamp turns on.

**Fig. 172**
BRAKE LAMP SWITCH

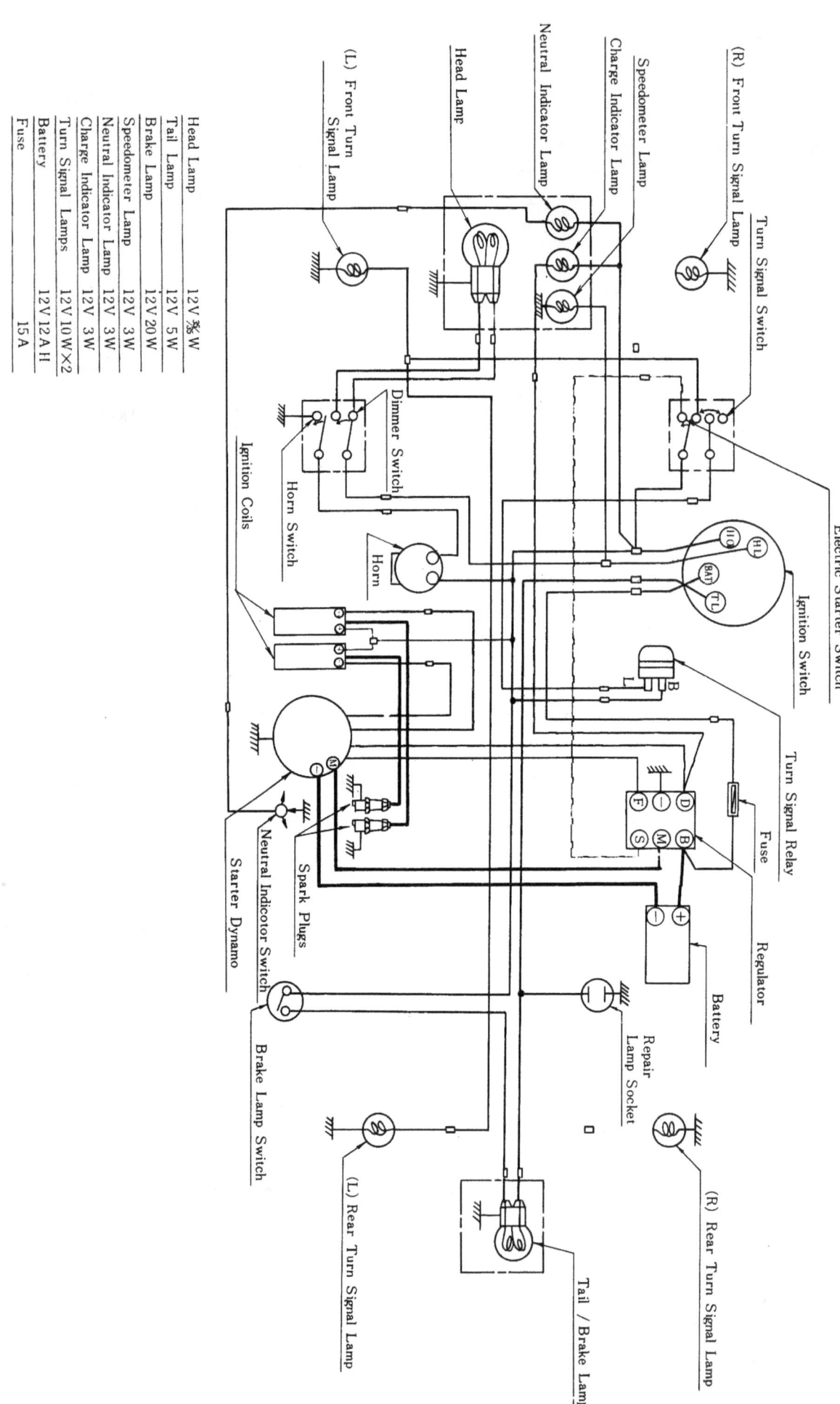

Wiring Diagram of Suzuki 250 Model T10

| Head Lamp | 12V 35W |
| Tail Lamp | 12V 5W |
| Brake Lamp | 12V 20W |
| Speedometer Lamp | 12V 3W |
| Neutral Indicator Lamp | 12V 3W |
| Charge Indicator Lamp | 12V 3W |
| Turn Signal Lamps | 12V 10W×2 |
| Battery | 12V 12AH |
| Fuse | 15A |

# SUZUKI MANUAL

## Book 2

Supplement to Book 1
(Model T10 and Basic Handbook)

# SUPPLEMENT TO SUZUKI 250 MODEL T10 SERVICE MANUAL

# 1. BRAKES IMPROVEMENT

Braking efficiency has been improved by installing a two leading shoe double cam brake on the front wheel and replacing the hydraulic rear brake with a mechanical brake for easier adjustment and maintenance, at the same time enlarging the size of both brake drums.

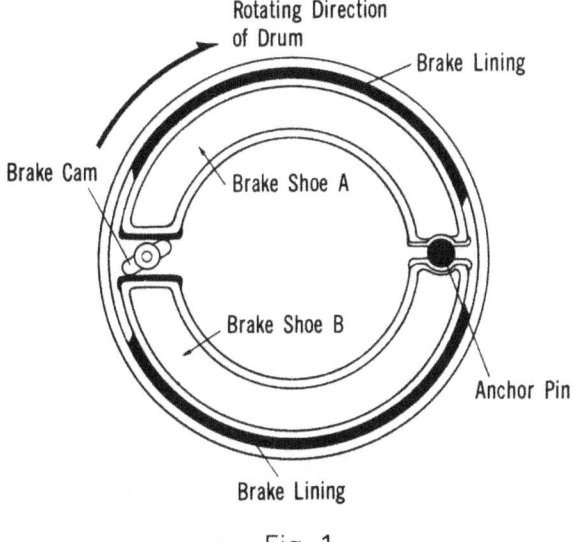

Fig. 1

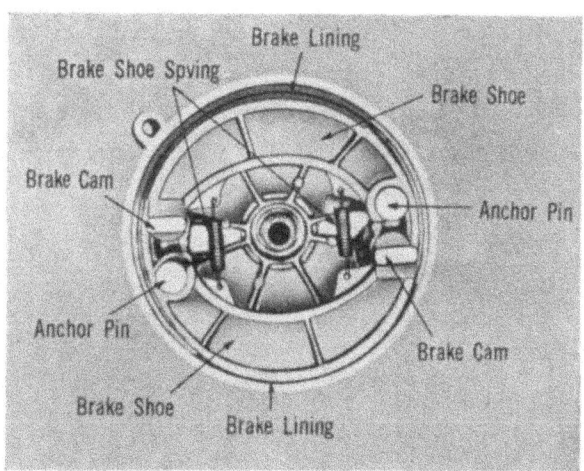

Fig. 2

## A. Two Leading Shoe Brake

When the brake is applied the cam turns and forces the brake shoe outward against the rotating brake drum. The turning force of the drum tries to move the brake shoe in the direction it is turning. This tendency is overcome by the anchor pin which holds brake shoe A, as shown in Fig. 1. Brake shoe B, however, is pushed against the partially turned brake cam, tending to force it back to the normal position and increasing the force required on the brake lever or brake pedal to keep the brake applied. Brake shoe A is called a leading shoe and brake shoe B is called a trailing shoe. In Fig. 2, which is a picture of the new front brake panel of model T10, there are two anchor pins and two brake cams, so that each brake shoe is a leading shoe. As the tendency to move with the rotating drum is stopped by an anchor pin in each shoe, neither pushes against the brake cam, making the action required to apply the brake very light. This type of brake is called a two leading shoe brake or, since there are two brake cams, a double cam brake.

## B. Brake Drum Size Enlarged

It requires less power to stop a rotating force of the same strength in a large diameter object than in an object of a smaller diameter. To increase brake efficiency, the size of both front and rear brake drums have been increased by 20 mm (0.787 in) in diameter.

## C. Brake Adjustment

### (1) Rear Brake

Since the rear brake drum has been enlarged, increasing braking efficiency, a hydraulic brake with its troublesome adjusting and maintenance problems is no longer necessary. Adjust play in the rear brake pedal to 20—30 mm (0.8—1.2 in) as in Fig. 3 with the brake rod adjusting nut on the brake rod, shown in Fig. 4.

### (2) Front Brake

a. Adjusting Brake Lever Play

Play in the brake lever is adjusted as on previous model T10 models. Adjust play so that the front brake begins to be applied when the brake lever is 20 mm (0.8 in) from the throttle grip with the brake calle adjuster shown in Fig. 5.

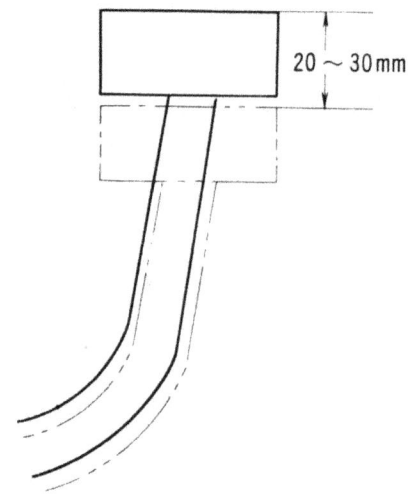

Fig. 3

Fig. 4

Fig. 5

b. Adjusting with Brake Lever Connector

Do not attempt to adjust the front brake with the brake lever connector except in the following cases only:

When worn brake linings have been replaced with new brake linings.

When front brake performance has become extremely bad and it is thought that only one brake shoe is contacting the drum.

Do not touch the brake lever connector except in these two cases.

Fig. 6

To abjust the brake with the lever connector in these two cases, refer to Fig. 6 and remove the brake cable adjusting nut and pull the brake cable from the brake cam lever.

Remove front axle nut and take out front axle.

Remove front hub panel from brake drum.

Loosen brake lever connector lock nut and turn the rod until both brake cams lay flat against the ends of the brake shoes.

Tighten the bake lever connector lock nut, fit thefront brake panel into the brake drum, insert the axle tighten the axle nut, fit the brake cable, screw on the brake cable adjusting nut and adjust the front brake lever.

## 2. STEERING DAMPER IMPROVEMENT

It is dangerous if the handlebar is turned suddenly when riding at high speeds, and difficult to ride on rough unpaved roads if the front wheel can swing from side to side freely.

To overcome these difficulties, the model T10 has had a friction type steering damper which is adjusted by hand with a knob.

This, however, required frequent and delicate adjustments by hand to fit the steering damper friction to road and riding conditions.

To make the motorcycle safer and easier to ride without the necessity of adjusting the steering damper, a hydraulic steering damper which works automatically to adjust steering stiffness to road and riding conditions and requires no adjustment has been fitted.

The hydraulic steering damper is held by the frame and connected to the bottom of the steering stem by a screw. (Fig. 7)

When the handlebar is turned, moving the steering stem, the damper guide screw connected to the steering stem is moved. (Fig. 8) The guide screw has grooves into which a large plate which acts as a piston is fitted. (Fig. 9) The piston is prevented from turning with the guide screw by a pin which holds it to the damper body.

When the guide screw turns, the piston is moved up and down by the grooves.

The inside of the damper case is filled with oil. There is one small hole in the piston.

When the piston moves up or down, the oil flows through this small hole. If the piston moves slowly, the oil flows through the hole smoothly with practically no resistance. If the piston moves rapidly, however, pressure is

Fig. 7

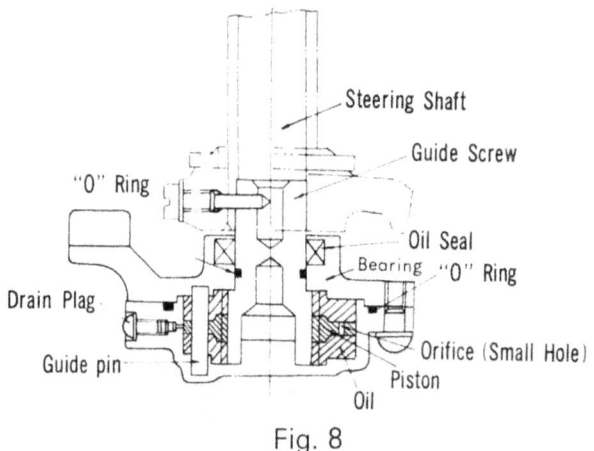

Fig. 8

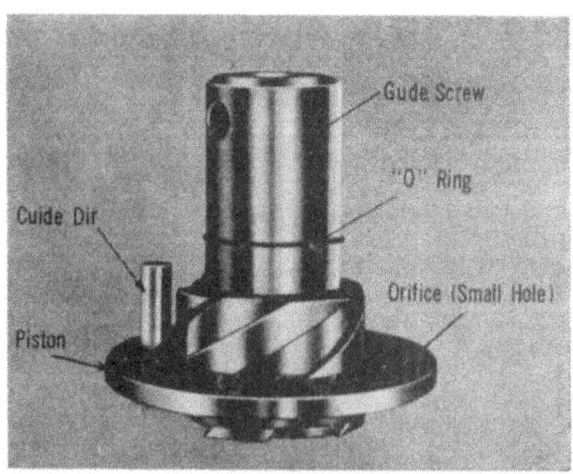

Fig. 9

built up because the oil cannot flow through the small hole fast enough and resistance to the movement of the piston increases rapidly. Since the damper is connected to the steering stem, resistance to the quick flopping of the front wheel from side to side is provided, preventing high speed wobbles or the wheel from being deflected by rocks or holes on bad roads.

## 3. REAR SHOCK ABSORBER IMPROVEMENT

Rear shock absorbers which can be adjusted to three stages to suit road and load conditions have been fitted. (Fig. 10)

Position 1 is for normal riding, position 2 is for high speeds or heavy loads and position 3 is for low speeds. The tension can be adjusted by turning the rear shock absorber lower cover with the cross head screw driver provided in the tool kit. Insert the handle end of the screw driver into the hole on the lower cover and turn it to right or left as shown in (Fig. 11)

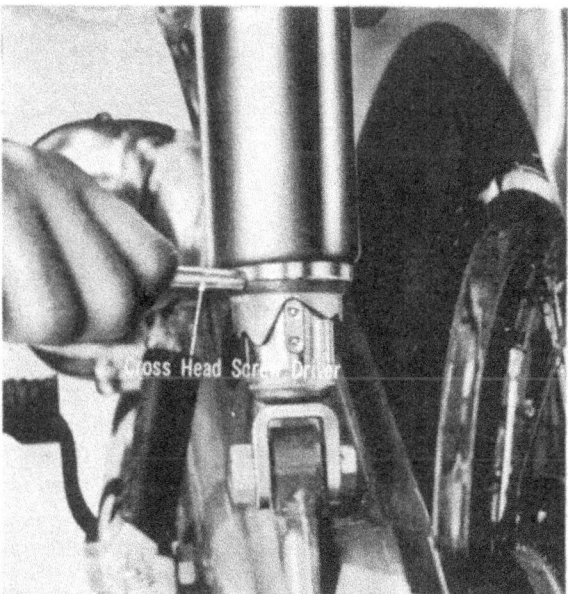

Fig. 10                                            Fig. 11

## 4. BALL END LEVERS

Safe ball end levers for clutch and front brake have been fitted. They also give a better appearing "sporty" look to the motorcycle. (Fig. 12)

## 5. WINDING TYPE THROTTLE

A racing type "quick throttle" in which the sliding piece is done away with and the throttle wire itself is wound around the throttle grip is fitted. The movement of the throttle grip is $\frac{1}{4}$ of a turn. (Fig. 12)

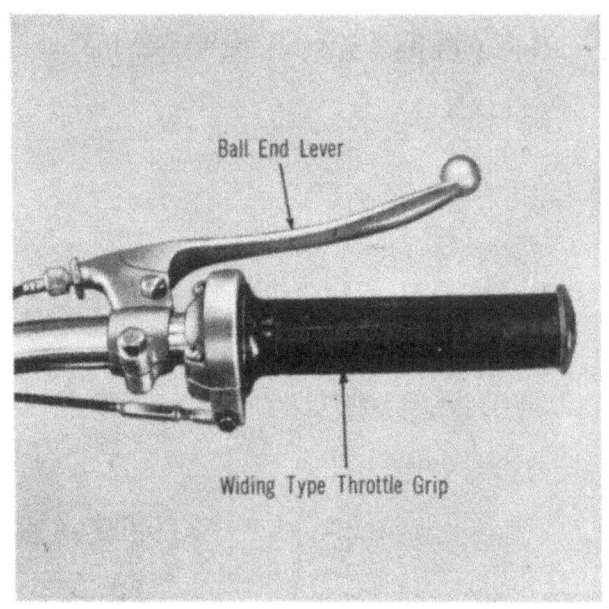

Fig. 12

## 6. HANDLEBAR SWITCH

The horn button and head lamp dimmer switch are all mounted on the left handlebar. (Fig. 13)

## 7. INTERCHANGABILITY OF PARTS

The new adjustable rear shock absorbers can be fitted to old models by replacing the lower fitting bolt. The other new parts, brakes, steering damper, ball end levers, throttle grip and switch, are not interchangable with those on old model motorcycles.

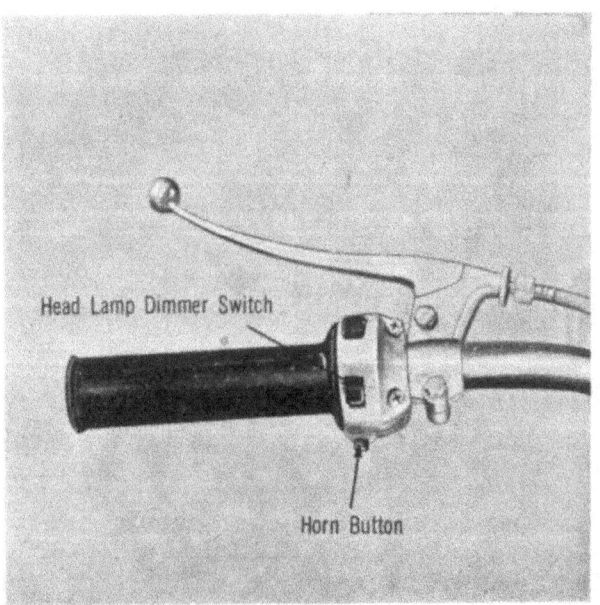

Fig. 13

## 8. CHANGE IN CARBURETOR SETTINGS

To improve performance at low engine speeds, for carburetor settings have been changed from engine number T10-16816, as listed below:

|  | Up to Engine No. T10-16815 | From Engine No. T10-16816 |
|---|---|---|
| Main Jet | 70 | 70 |
| Air Jet | 1.3 | 1.3 |
| Jet Needle | **24 A -4 th groove** | **24 A -2 nd groove** |
| Needle Jet | N-6 | N-6 |
| Cutaway | 2.5 | 3.0 |
| Pilot Jet | #30 | #40 |
| Bypass | 1.4 | 1.4 |
| Pilot Outlet | 0.6 | 0.6 |
| Air Screw | 1½ turns back | 2 turns back |
| Valve Seat | 2.0 | 2.0 |

## A SAMPLE LIST OF OTHER BOOKS AVAILABLE FROM

## www.VelocePress.com

## PLEASE CHECK OUR WEBSITE FOR THE MOST UP-TO-DATE INFORMATION

### MOTORCYCLE WORKSHOP MANUALS, MAINTENANCE & TECHNICAL TITLES

**ARIEL** WORKSHOP MANUAL 1933-1951
**BMW** FACTORY WORKSHOP MANUAL R26 R27 (1956-1967)
**BMW** FACTORY WSM R50 R50S R60 R69S R50US R60US R69US (1955-1969)
**BSA** SERVICE & REPAIR ALL PRE-WAR MODELS TO 1939, SV & OHV 150cc TO 1,000cc
**DUCATI** FACTORY WORKSHOP MANUAL SINGLE CYLINDER NARROW CASE OHC ENGINES 160cc, 250cc, 350cc - MONZA JUNIOR, MONZA, 250GT, MARK 3, MACH 1, MOTOCROSS & SEBRING
**HONDA** FACTORY WORKSHOP MANUAL 250cc TO 305cc C/CS/CB 72 & 77 SERIES 1960-1969
**HONDA** SERVICE & REPAIR 50cc TO 305cc C100, C102, MONKEY BIKE, CE 105H TRIALS BIKE, C110, C114, C92, CB92, BENLEY, C72, CB72, C77 & CB77
**NORTON** FACTORY WORKSHOP MANUAL 1957-1970
**NORTON** WORKSHOP MANUAL 1932-1939
**ROYAL ENFIELD** 736cc INTERCEPTOR & ENFIELD INDIAN CHIEF
**SUZUKI T10** FACTORY WORKSHOP MANUAL 250cc 1963-1967
**SUZUKI T20 & T200** FACTORY WORKSHOP MANUAL 200cc X-5 INVADER & STING RAY SCRAMBLER, 250cc X-6 HUSTLER 1965-1969
**TRIUMPH** FACTORY WORKSHOP MANUAL NO. 11 (1945-1955)
**TRIUMPH** WORKSHOP MANUAL 1935-1939
**TRIUMPH** WORKSHOP MANUAL 1937-1951
**VESPA** SERVICE & REPAIR ALL MODELS 125cc & 150cc 1951-1961
**VINCENT** SERVICE & REPAIR 1935-1955

### CLASSIC AUTO TITLES & REFERENCE BOOKS

**ABARTH** BUYERS GUIDE
**CARRERA PANAMERICANA 1950** ~ THE STORY OF THE 1950 MEXICAN ROAD RACE
**DIALED IN** ~ THE JAN OPPERMAN STORY
**FERRARI** 308 SERIES BUYER'S AND OWNER'S GUIDE
**FERRARI** BERLINETTA LUSSO
**FERRARI** BROCHURES & SALES LITERATURE 1946-1967
**FERRARI** SERIAL NUMBERS PART I ~ STREET CARS TO SERIAL # 21399 (1948-1977)
**FERRARI** SERIAL NUMBERS PART II ~ RACE CARS TO SERIAL # 1050 (1948-1973)
**FERRARI** SPYDER CALIFORNIA
**IF HEMINGWAY HAD WRITTEN A RACING NOVEL** ~ THE BEST OF MOTOR RACING FICTION 1950-2000
**LE MANS 24** ~ WHAT THE MOVIE COULD HAVE BEEN
**MASERATI** BROCHURES AND SALES LITERATURE ~ POSTWAR THROUGH INLINE 6 CYLINDER CARS

All VelocePress titles are available through your local independent bookseller, Amazon.com, or they may be purchased directly through our website at www.VelocePress.com. Wholesale customers may also purchase directly from us or from the Ingram Book Group.

## OTHER WORKSHOP MANUALS, MAINTENANCE & TECHNICAL TITLES

**AUSTIN HEALEY** SIX CYLINDER CARS 1956-1968
**BMW** ISETTA FACTORY REPAIR MANUAL
**FERRARI** 250/GT SERVICE AND MAINTENANCE
**FERRARI** GUIDE TO PERFORMANCE
**FERRARI** OPERATING, MAINTENANCE & SERVICE HANDBOOKS 1948-1963
**FERRARI** OWNER'S HANDBOOK
**FERRARI** TUNING TIPS & MAINTENANCE TECHNIQUES
**MASERATI** OWNER'S HANDBOOK
**OBERT'S FIAT GUIDE**
**PERFORMANCE TUNING THE SUNBEAM TIGER**
**PORSCHE 356** SERVICE AND MAINTENANCE MANUAL 1948-1965
**PORSCHE 912** WORKSHOP MANUAL
**SOUPING THE VOLKSWAGEN** IMPROVING THE PERFORMANCE OF YOUR VW
**TRIUMPH TR2, TR3 & TR4** WORKSHOP MANUAL
**VOLVO** ALL MODELS 1944-1968 WORKSHOP MANUAL

## BROOKLANDS ROAD TEST PORTFOLIOS

**FIAT DINO** 1968-1973
**MV AGUSTA F4** 750 & 1000 1997-2007
**JAGUAR MK1 & MK2** 1955-1969
**LOTUS CORTINA** 1963-1970
**FIAT 500** 1936-1972

All VelocePress titles are available through your local independent bookseller, Amazon.com, or they may be purchased directly through our website at www.VelocePress.com. Wholesale customers may also purchase directly from us or from the Ingram Book Group.

## AUTOBOOKS SERIES OF WORKSHOP MANUALS

**ALFA ROMEO** GIULIA 1750, 2000 1962-1978 WORKSHOP MANUAL
**AUSTIN HEALEY** SPRITE, MG MIDGET 1958-1980 WORKSHOP MANUAL
**BMW** 1600 1966-1973 WORKSHOP MANUAL
**FIAT** 1100, 1100D, 1100R & 1200 1957-1969 WORKSHOP MANUAL
**FIAT** 124 1966-1974 WORKSHOP MANUAL
**FIAT** 124 SPORT 1966-1975 WORKSHOP MANUAL
**FIAT** 125 & 125 SPECIAL 1967-1973 WORKSHOP MANUAL
**FIAT** 126, 126L, 126DV, 126/650 & 126/650DV 1972-1982 WORKSHOP MANUAL
**FIAT** 127 SALOON, SPECIAL & SPORT, 900, 1050 1971-1981 WORKSHOP MANUAL
**FIAT** 128 1969-1982 WORKSHOP MANUAL
**FIAT** 1300, 1500 1961-1967 WORKSHOP MANUAL
**FIAT** 131 MIRAFIORI 1975-1982 WORKSHOP MANUAL
**FIAT** 132 1972-1982 WORKSHOP MANUAL
**FIAT** 500 1957-1973 WORKSHOP MANUAL
**FIAT** 600, 600D & MULTIPLA 1955-1969 WORKSHOP MANUAL
**FIAT** 850 1964-1972 WORKSHOP MANUAL
**JAGUAR** E-TYPE 1961-1972 WORKSHOP MANUAL
**JAGUAR** MK 1, 2 1955-1969 WORKSHOP MANUAL
**JAGUAR** S TYPE, 420 1963-1968 WORKSHOP MANUAL
**JAGUAR** XK 120, 140, 150 MK 7, 8, 9 1948-1961 WORKSHOP MANUAL
**LAND ROVER** 1, 2 1948-1961 WORKSHOP MANUAL
**MERCEDES-BENZ** 190 1959-1968 WORKSHOP MANUAL
**MERCDEDS-BENZ** 220/8 1968-1972 WORKSHOP MANUAL
**MERCEDES-BENZ** 230 1963-1968 WORKSHOP MANUAL
**MERCEDES-BENZ** 250 1968-1972 WORKSHOP MANUAL
**MG** MIDGET TA-TF 1936-1955 WORKSHOP MANUAL
**MINI** 1959-1980 WORKSHOP MANUAL
**MORRIS** MINOR 1952-1971 WORKSHOP MANUAL
**PEUGEOT** 404 1960-1975 WORKSHOP MANUAL
**PORSCHE** 911 1964-1969 WORKSHOP MANUAL
**PORSCHE** 911 1970-1977 WORKSHOP MANUAL
**RENAULT** 8, 10, 1100 1962-1971 WORKSHOP MANUAL
**RENAULT** 16 1965-1979 WORKSHOP MANUAL
**ROVER** 3500, 3500S 1968-1976 WORKSHOP MANUAL
**SUNBEAM** RAPIER, ALPINE 1955-1965 WORKSHOP MANUAL
**TRIUMPH** SPITFIRE, GT6, VITESSE 1962-1968 WORKSHOP MANUAL
**TRIUMPH** TR2, TR3, TR3A 1952-1962 WORKSHOP MANUAL
**TRIUMPH** TR4, TR4A 1961-1967 WORKSHOP MANUAL
**VOLKSWAGEN** BEETLE 1968-1977 WORKSHOP MANUAL

**All VelocePress titles are available through your local independent bookseller, Amazon.com, or they may be purchased directly through our website at www.VelocePress.com. Wholesale customers may also purchase directly from us or from the Ingram Book Group.**

www.ingramcontent.com/pod-product-compliance
Lightning Source LLC
Chambersburg PA
CBHW080924170426
43201CB00016B/2254